New Directions for Adult and Continuing Education

Susan Imel
Jovita M. Ross-Gordon
Joellen E. Coryell
COEDITORS-IN-CHIEF

Swimming Up Stream 2: Agency and Urgency in the Education of Black Men

Brendaly Drayton
Dionne Rosser-Mims
Joni Schwartz
Talmadge C. Guy

EDITORS

Number 150 • Summer 2016
Jossey-Bass
San Francisco

Swimming Up Stream 2: Agency and Urgency in the Education of Black Men
Brendaly Drayton, Dionne Rosser-Mims, Joni Schwartz, Talmadge C. Guy (eds.)
New Directions for Adult and Continuing Education, no. 150
Susan Imel, Jovita M. Ross-Gordon, and Joellen E. Coryell Coeditors-in-Chief

Microfilm copies of issues and articles are available in 16mm and 35mm, as well as microfiche in 105mm, through University Microfilms Inc., 300 North Zeeb Road, Ann Arbor, Michigan 48106-1346.

NEW DIRECTIONS FOR ADULT AND CONTINUING EDUCATION (ISSN 1052-2891, electronic ISSN 1536-0717) is part of The Jossey-Bass Higher and Adult Education Series and is published quarterly by Wiley Subscription Services, Inc., A Wiley Company, at Jossey-Bass, One Montgomery Street, Suite 1200, San Francisco, CA 94104-4594. POSTMASTER: Send address changes to New Directions for Adult and Continuing Education, Jossey-Bass, One Montgomery Street, Suite 1200, San Francisco, CA 94104-4594.

New Directions for Adult and Continuing Education is indexed in CIJE: Current Index to Journals in Education (ERIC); Contents Pages in Education (T&F); ERIC Database (Education Resources Information Center); Higher Education Abstracts (Claremont Graduate University); and Sociological Abstracts (CSA/CIG).

INDIVIDUAL SUBSCRIPTION RATE (in USD): $89 per year US/Can/Mex, $113 rest of world; institutional subscription rate: $335 US, $375 Can/Mex, $409 rest of world. Single copy rate: $29. Electronic only–all regions: $89 individual, $335 institutional; Print & Electronic–US: $98 individual, $402 institutional; Print & Electronic–Canada/Mexico: $98 individual, $442 institutional; Print & Electronic–Rest of World: $122 individual, $476 institutional.

EDITORIAL CORRESPONDENCE should be sent to the Coeditors-in-Chief, Susan Imel, 3076 Woodbine Place, Columbus, Ohio 43202-1341, e-mail: imel.1@osu.edu; or Jovita M. Ross-Gordon, Texas State University, CLAS Dept., 601 University Drive, San Marcos, TX 78666; Joellen E. Coryell, Texas State University, 601 University Drive, ASBS Room 326 San Marcos, TX 78666-4616.

Cover design: Wiley
Cover Images: © Lava 4 images | Shutterstock

www.josseybass.com

CONTENTS

EDITORS' NOTES

This volume of *New Directions for Adult and Continuing Education* titled "Swimming Up Stream 2: Agency and Urgency in the Education of Black Men" is a continuation of a two-part series that focuses on salient topics and issues affecting Black males as they engage in adult education and learning. In the first volume, "Swimming Upstream: Black Males and Adult Education," we used the analogy of the annual salmon run to describe the obstacles Black men confront in the daily struggle to lead meaningful and productive lives (Guy, 2014). We presented the voices and experiences of Black men through a variety of topics, including reentry adult college students, the role of trauma in the lives of young men, fatherhood, the formerly incarcerated, vets and the GI bill, and the GED® setting as a counterspace for early negative schooling experiences. We began the volume by laying the sociohistorical foundations for the current experiences of Black men today and ended with a call to action.

Like the first volume, this book assumes that both the historical and current social contexts of learning have a unique impact on the way in which Black men engage in adult education. The chapter selections advance the conversations around adult Black males' educational experiences by using academic research as well as program descriptions and personal narratives with a concern for the "lived experiences" and voices of the men. It focuses on pathways to achievement using multiple contexts and individual, institutional, and societal perspectives. More specifically, we explore the agency of Black men in carving out pathways to success, the programs that support these endeavors, and the role of civil society in facilitating or inhibiting their progress.

Through the different perspectives and voices represented in this volume, we continue to address issues facing Black men in adult education and challenge commonly held stereotypes, interactions, and policies. This current volume addresses such topics as the Black Lives Matter movement, the digital divide, sports, professional career development, sexuality, role of religion, Black male initiative programs, and college as a choice. The book is designed to raise questions about the distinctive experiences of this specific population and to explore the sociocultural dynamics that affect their education and learning. It also serves as a reminder that practitioners must regularly reflect on their own practices as they work toward increased engagement of Black men in learning communities and develop ways to support the personal and professional development of these men as adult learners.

The Editors

We, the editors, wish to briefly reflect on what influenced each of us to come together to give "voice" to the lived experiences of adult Black males in the

NEW DIRECTIONS FOR ADULT AND CONTINUING EDUCATION, no. 150, Summer 2016 © 2016 Wiley Periodicals, Inc.
Published online in Wiley Online Library (wileyonlinelibrary.com) • DOI: 10.1002/ace.20181

context of adult education. Our individual stories, respective positionalities, and deep concern for Black men's educational development converge in our scholarship as follows:

Talmadge C. Guy. "Where are the men?" I ask. As a Black man, it would seem natural to dwell on issues affecting Black men in today's world. Actually, I was quite mature before I even began to think of this as a problem. I clearly remember in 1985 reading the cover page of a popular magazine asking about the disappearing species of Black males. I recall saying to myself that Black men aren't disappearing. They're right here. They were not a vanishing species but instead were actually quite numerous. It was that they were not in school or at work—at least in the conventional sense.

Existentially, I have a great disdain for men, but I suppose especially Black men, who are unable to "take care of their business," meaning not taking care of himself, his family, supporting the community where feasible, and so on. At the same time, I completely recognize how institutional racism negatively affects Black males. I see it directly, experience it, and know about it through an examination of the literature.

What is relevant in terms of our project is how "late" it is in the evolution of the literature on race and gender that the experiences of Black men are put forward. I feel a kind of "double bind" because many of our sisters have effectively and passionately described, documented, and theorized the condition and experiences of Black women. The bind consists in the desire to give women their space, while at the same time pushing for more space to hear the voices of Black men. Too often, these two impulses seem in tension with each other. To assert the problems associated with Black men anticipates a kind of male privilege—or does it? I don't think so because the problems faced by so many Black women are correlated with the problems faced by Black men. I think that's true. I feel it is a controversial and perhaps contentious issue with some of our sisters. The double bind is a tough place in which to reside. But I'm pleased that in this series we have "opened space" to give expression to a conversation that is long overdue.

Joni Schwartz. Since 1982 I have worked (with great delight) in the field of adult education in many settings, such as grassroots community-based organizations and community organizing, faith-based initiatives, research, and community college. Through and during the era of the war on drugs, inception of the AIDS epidemic, welfare reform, No Child Left Behind, the legal resegregation of public schools, mass incarceration of Black males, and now urban gentrification, I have worked in the field with hundreds of young men of color who have mainly dropped out of school to seek a high school equivalency diploma through one of the three adult education centers I developed, with the Black Male Initiative STEM program that I coordinated, or with those who have made their way to the community college where I teach. These young men are my friends, my colleagues, my mentors, my mentees, my students, my God-sons, my co-writers and participatory action research partners.

In 2000 while still working full time developing and directing an adult education center, I began my doctoral program in adult education. It was this journey along the subsequent 10 years that focused me on young men of color in adult education. A dissertation committee member at the time asked me "What do you care about? What are you passionate about?"—this is what you need to do your research on. I knew I cared about the engagement in learning of Bryant, Kareem, John, Jovon, Keanu, Brian, Felipe, Jerry, Kaleem, and many others. So I chose this topic, which made the research and dissertation process both engaging and very painful. It was during the dissertation process that my very personal understanding of this topic would converge with the statistics and broader historical/structural issues around men of color and their education. This convergence would be transformative, confusing, heartbreaking, and deeply troubling. For the first time, I would understand my positionality as a White female adult educator in a new way. I continue to this day to grapple with this positionality as I live, research, write, and continually *unpack* my interest convergence, responsibility, and privilege.

Brendaly Drayton. My interest in Black men and education was awakened by varied experiences (Drayton, 2012). Assumptions that early school leavers were not interested in learning or had cognitive problems were challenged by two young men I met at an adult literacy program. One was a gifted writer and the other had an affinity for math. Both passed the GED® without a problem. This did not make sense to me—a disorienting dilemma, if you will. Why were they in a GED® program instead of finishing high school? Furthermore, the student who was the gifted writer co-taught a math class with me after passing the GED®, and I noticed he had a connection with the students and garnered their attention. It was a connection I had not tapped into that was based on similar experiences and understandings.

My involvement with the adult literacy program sensitized me to topics in the media concerning Black males in education. I recalled seeing newspaper headlines that said more than 50% of Black males were going to jail and over 40% were dropping out of school. These outcomes also did not make sense to me and I wanted to understand the contributing factors. The media had probably addressed this topic before; however, my background in the business sectors had blinded me to these circumstances. During my journey as a graduate student, I discovered that there was sparse research on Black men in adult literacy programs yet they were considered "hard to reach." My interaction with adult learners and research indicate that program participation was a means for adult learners to bring about positive change in their lives. The question that arose for me was how can we, as adult educators, engage them if we do not have an understanding of their daily lived experiences? I wondered about the young men's undiscovered talents that were lost to their communities and more broadly to our society. It reminded of the scripture verse, "Much food is in the tilled land of the poor, but they are those who are destroyed because of injustice" (Proverbs, 13:23, Amplified Bible).

Therefore, my dissertation and research have focused on Black men and their educational experiences. In order to provide programs that take into consideration Black men's needs, we must understand the issues from their perspectives. The Adult Education Research Conference offered a venue for meeting like-minded individuals who shared a belief that Black men's voices and experiences needed to be heard to affect positive change in their educational experiences and by extension their daily lived experiences in society. The first volume, *Swimming Upstream: Black Men and Adult Education*, was a first step in advancing that initiative.

Dionne Rosser-Mims. My story begins with "Where is David?," a single father who I convinced to return to college but could not retain. Although all of us may face troubling times or various degrees of adversity, there are those currently on the campuses of colleges and universities across the nation whose very presence in the college classroom symbolizes an educational and cultural transformation. This aptly reflects the experiences of the adult Black male first-generation or reentry college students. These are people bound by a multiplicity of circumstances. All share a desire to better themselves, serve as a role model for their family and community, and see education as a means to enhance their lives. It is with this belief in mind that I was motivated to create in 2009 an outreach initiative titled the Parent Degree Program (PDP) intended to increase the number of parents with school-age children who hold a college degree. From the start of the PDP most of the parents who participated were Black females. The first male to join the PDP support network was one of the few students I was unable to retain. The multiple attempts I made to reach David to encourage him to return were unsuccessful. As a Black female with a passion for the underserved, this bothered me greatly. I began to even question what I should have done differently to support him and, more broadly, other adult Black male college students to mitigate the structural barriers that curtail access to college and even success as reentry college students. What changes at the institutional level should be made to support this segment of the student population? I have made it my mission to find ways to claim, reclaim, and retain other men like "David" who may be out there. This was the impetus for the chapter I co-authored in the first volume of this sourcebook concerning reentry adult Black male college students.

Chapter Summaries

Since the publication of our first volume, we have witnessed, and in some cases, participated in civil protests in Atlanta, Baltimore, New York, Ferguson, Missouri, as well as other major cities across the country in response to the tragic deaths of Black males, such as Freddie Gray, Eric Gardner, and Michael Brown. We make the case that the tragic occurrences of these men's deaths and subsequent civil unrest are not unrelated to issues of educational equity and education as a civil right. It is with this understanding that we posit the Black Lives Matter movement must address multiple layers of intervention and change from broad police, education, incarceration, economic, and health policies affecting our nation to individual classroom and practitioner interventions. Therefore, in light of these occurrences, it seems essential for adult educators to acknowledge the recent tragic events as deeply related to adult education practice and to reexamine the structural dynamics present in our classrooms, practices, and activism.

An underlying theme of this volume is that injustice and inequity in various forms devalue certain lives through the structural barriers and policies that restrict pathways to improving quality of life. Consequently, the opening chapter of this volume, "Black Lives Matter and Adult Education: One Community College Initiative," highlights this issue. It begins with a quotation from the first author that we believe reflects the historical and current experience of Black men in the United States and underpins the significance of this identity marker in all the chapters. In this first chapter, Brian Miller and Joni Schwartz share lessons learned from a community college initiative that served as a way for students, faculty, and college leadership to process the unrest we see across the country. Particular emphasis is placed on exploring the importance of pedagogy, community, and scholarly activism as a vehicle for social change.

Simone C. O. Conceição and Larry Martin in Chapter 2, titled "Black Men and the Digital Divide," address the ongoing technological, economic, and social changes Black men face due to the proverbial digital divide. They extend the discussion to offer recommendations on how adult educators can help these men successfully navigate the digital divide. In Chapter 3, Richard Osborne and Joni Schwartz engage in a provocative dialogue around factors that influence Black men's decision whether to attend or not to attend college. The authors explore alternative pathways to success like entrepreneurism and the role that self-directed learning plays.

The next two chapters focus on the significant educational role that Black churches have historically played in the Black community and therefore in the lives of Black men. Chapter 4, titled "Black Males in Black Churches," underscores the important historical and contemporary role of Black churches as adult education agencies that support the Black community and in particular Black men's educational, social, and leadership development. Traci Hodges, Michael Rowland, and E. Paulette Isaac Savage identify church-based programs as examples of programs and initiatives that have successfully responded to this population's needs. In Chapter 5, Lawrence Bryant, Lorenzo Bowman, and E. Paulette Isaac Savage highlight the insider/outsider issues precipitated by positionality (Merriam et al., 2001). They also discuss the intersection of Black gay men and spirituality through the use of autoethnographic data, as well as explore alternate meaning making strategies in the face of oppositional dominant ideologies in Black communities and churches.

Chapters 6 and 7 focus on life beyond college and career development from different venues, respectively. In Chapter 6, "Academic and Career Advancement for Black Male Athletes at NCAA Division I Institutions," Ashley Baker and Billy Hawkins explore the social, educational, and economic implications for sport being positioned as a viable means for upward social mobility for Black males who come from lower socioeconomic circumstances. Moving from the context of the sports to corporate America, Tonya Harris Cornileus in Chapter 7, "The Brotherhood in Corporate America," offers a cogent discussion on the lived experiences of 14 Black professional men and how their race and gender identities, and the overarching assumption of male privilege in corporate America, have affected their career development experiences.

In the closing chapter, "Swimming into the Open," we highlight themes that emerged in the chapters of this volume and hope to inspire the readers like you to take action through research agendas, the creation of venues for discussion, and the establishing and promoting of initiatives that foster the educational and social well-being of Black men and in essence demonstrates that Black Lives Matter.

Acknowledgements

It has been both an honor and a privilege to work with the authors of this volume toward expanding the literature base on the topic of Black males in adult education. We extend a special thank you to Mardie McIlmoyl and Neoma Mullins for their editorial assistance.

Brendaly Drayton
Dionne Rosser-Mims
Joni Schwartz
Talmadge C. Guy
Editors

References

Drayton, B. (2012). *Literacy and identity: Reflections of six African-American males in an adult literacy program* (Doctoral dissertation). Available from ProQuest Dissertations and Theses database. (UMI No. 3534656)

Guy, T. (2014). The (End)angered Black male swimming against the current. In D. Rosser-Mims, J. Schwartz, B. Drayton, & T. Guy (Eds.), *New Directions for Adult and Continuing Education: No. 144. Swimming upstream: Black males in adult education.* (pp. 15–26). San Francisco, CA: Jossey-Bass.

Merriam, S., Johnson-Bailey, J., Lee, M., Kee, Y., Ntseane, G., & Muhamad, M. (2001). Power and positionality: Negotiating insider/outsider status within and across cultures. *International Journal of Lifelong Education, 20*(5), 405–416.

BRENDALY DRAYTON *is the coordinator of the Guided Study Groups program and an adult education instructor at The Pennsylvania State University.*

DIONNE ROSSER-MIMS *is an associate professor and assistant department chair in the Department of Leadership Development and Professional Studies at Troy University.*

JONI SCHWARTZ is an associate professor in the Humanities Department at LaGuardia Community College, City University of New York.

TALMADGE C. GUY is an associate professor of adult education at the University of Georgia.

New Directions for Adult and Continuing Education • DOI: 10.1002/ace

1

This chapter is a call to action for adult educators to critically engage the Black Lives Matter Movement through pedagogy, community engagement and scholarly activism. It explores the intersection of the Black Lives Matter movement and adult education by highlighting the response of one community college initiative.

The Intersection of Black Lives Matter and Adult Education: One Community College Initiative

Brian Miller, Joni Schwartz

I (Brian) am currently a student and had the privilege of delivering a speech before a community college Black Lives Matters Summit. During my introduction I uttered these words:

> I come before you today . . . .not as a Democrat or a Republican, not as a conservative or a liberal, not as a Tea Partier, or an Occupier . . . . But as the only thing I KNOW that I am, as the only thing that AMERICA WILL NEVER LET ME FORGET THAT I AM . . . A BLACK MAN!

The audience seemed to resonate with my statement. I later added, "We are not suggesting that all lives do not matter, but right now we are talking about *Black* lives." This clarification was meant not to be disparaging or dismissive of any other race, instead to underscore that there is no other group in the United States that is being systematically targeted and murdered as routinely as Black males—a concern that has garnered national and international attention and warranted a movement recognized by both Blacks, Whites, and other racial groups (Gabrielson, Jones, & Sagara, 2014). This movement is designed both to bring public awareness to a very real problem and also to encourage Americans to stand and act in solidarity to preserve the dignity and frankly the lives of all Blacks but particularly Black males.

This particular call to action and engagement took place at the first annual Black Lives Matter Summit at LaGuardia Community College (LAGCC)-City University of New York, which was both a community and college event;

NEW DIRECTIONS FOR ADULT AND CONTINUING EDUCATION, no. 150, Summer 2016 © 2016 Wiley Periodicals, Inc.
Published online in Wiley Online Library (wileyonlinelibrary.com) • DOI: 10.1002/ace.20182

although resonating with some, it disturbed and agitated others. Anonymous email responses included the following sentiments: "All lives matter, asshole." And "We should not single out groups. Some Black men are just criminals, plain and simple. Michael Brown and Trayvon Martin would not have died if they did not flee or commit crimes or look like they were committing crimes." Another anonymous individual registered his disagreement by stating "In America, White lives matter," and still another individual explained that if Black people want to live better lives they should "get jobs and stop breaking laws like other Americans."

Although seeming to be intentionally offensive, these comments expose subtler themes of value and white privilege (Rasmussen Reports, 2015). These paradigms with the accompanying sentiments seem to highlight that there is a premium and privilege on White life that both society as a political actor recognizes and laws protect and adjudicate (Culp, 1998; McIntosh, 1988).

There is, was, and continues to be no need in the United States to endorse Whiteness as a valued feature and social position of American life or citizenship, whereas Blacks are still grappling with the reality that the law and policy has generally not been written to protect, but to oppress. This is what DuBois (1903) called the double consciousness of the Black man in America; this is the awareness of two identities in conflict: the American who is also the Black man. The Black man, though American, is not given the full benefits and rights of being a citizen of this country, and on an even larger scale there is a denial of his humanity (DuBois, 1903), which forces him all too often to operate from a deficit model and assume a role of inferiority (Gorski, 2011).

The point in this chapter is to call *you*, the adult educator and student, to action. If you haven't already, we encourage you to challenge your perceptions and to challenge those around you to pedagogically as well as critically engage this movement in this moment. We begin by discussing the Black man's positionality in America and the foundations of Black solidarity and then move to discuss the birth of the Black Lives Matter movement. From there we investigate the intersection of adult education and Black Lives Matter, including an example of one response by a community college.

Foundations of Black Solidarity

When the authors of this chapter use the term *Black*, we are employing its meaning by defining it in the context of a social construction not a phenotypical derivation (Omi & Winant, 1994; Sheared, Johnson-Bailey, Colin, Peterson, & Brookfield, 2010; Smedley & Smedley, 2005). Furthermore, we posit that the Black Lives Movement at its foundation draws from a philosophical framework credited to Tommie Shelby and his explanation of collective oppression or collective identity as a "means of understanding Black solidarity given the fact there is no pure race" (Shelby, 2002, p. 244). The collective feelings of oppression, treatment, discrimination, and racism serve as social indicators of status, defining both privilege and contempt; these markers serve as acceptable and reliable identifiers of race and thus discrimination, creating the foundation for a shared identity. "They [Blacks] suffer the same or collective form of racial subordination [thus giving them a] ... common interest in ending racial inequality" (Shelby, 2002, p. 247). Most often this collective begins to feel a sense of commonality with others who are facing similar oppression. It is by this yoke of oppression that those who suffer under these feelings of oppression form alliances and shared feelings of identity. This belief is notable in that it reflects not only in those who find themselves oppressed but can happen with those who find themselves privileged. Therein it is possible to conceive of a solidarity of privilege for Whites. This identification of shared privilege and understanding of whiteness may very well be the beginning of education toward solidarity with oppressed groups and the embracing of antiracist, ally positionality (Johnson-Bailey & Cervero, 1998; Shore, 2001). It is from this framework that we discuss the concept of race.

The question of *race* and thus the othering of those not in the dominant social group is one that has to be both created and accepted by the oppressor and oppressed, constructing social identity and thus *race*. This process of stratification separates subordinate groups from the dominant groups. It is these constructions of identities that allow for the systematic discrimination of those who lack political or social power; in effect, these social markers are then used to "justify the ill treatment and deplorable condition of the subordinate group" (Shelby, 2002, p. 247). These classifications and fictitious categories are created for the purpose of social control and the creation of a tiered value system that reinforces the stereotypical falsehoods being offered by the oppressive groups (Alexander, 2010). *Blackness* is an ideological construct much "like many such constructs including nation and ethnicity it is extremely malleable and capacious" (Shelby, 2002, p. 254), constantly changing and morphing to fit the constraints of the time period in which the injustice is being committed.

Birth of Black Lives Matter

Out of this philosophical foundation and the collective sense of injustice and desperation, the Black Lives Matter movement was spawned; it was the brainchild of three courageous women who are self-proclaimed Black activists: Alicia Garza, Patrisse Cullors, and Opal Tometi (Valentina, 2015). All three women desired political and social redress for the lives stolen by police and citizen vigilantes (Ross, 2015). The movement initially came to the fore after the acquittal of George Zimmerman, who shot and killed 17-year-old Trayvon Martin. To many in the African American community this loss was more than a loss; it was the embodiment of injustice and illegitimacy. It is *this* lived experience of injustice, *this* perception of the illegitimacy of the justice system that has caused protesters to form on the streets and demand justice. The experience of injustice led to frustration and from frustration to anger, not even necessarily about Trayvon Martin (or later Mike Brown's death) but from anticipating the verdict before it was announced. There was an expectation that these incidents would end "the way it usually does" for the African American community; this was more than a boy dying, this was *ANOTHER* boy dying (Gabrielson, Jones, & Sagara, 2014).

These acquittals are a rebuke to the Black community and affirmation of the insignificance of Black life, proving that not all life has the same value as that of *other true* citizens. Through and through this perception of the guilt of the victim and guilt of the Black male body is seen as formal injustice. To these communities of color there is an underlying political unchanging hypocritical reality of American life extending beyond the threshold of unfairness, stretching back to the founding of the country, a complication of history that proves not only that the system is not fair, but that the system is designed to be unfair as it is a direct outgrowth of White supremacy.

Nowhere is this reality more present than in the policing of the nondominant group. One response to this formal injustice is "spontaneous rebellion ... (including, but not limited to) expressing contempt for authority ... vandalizing public and private property, or disrupting public events ... culminating in the formation of urban riot(s) where looting, mass destruction, and brutal violence are on full display" (Shelby, 2002, p. 257), which can become the order of the day.

These sometimes violent behaviors fail to ensure a political outcome that best serves the community but allow those engaged to come to voice and feel a sense of self-respect. With that said, it may not be that violence is the most appropriate course of action, but it is an understandable one. My wise father once explained to me (Brian) that "this life just ain't fair, for men of color it's even worse, it's unjust, a wise man learns and knows that justice is a requisite for peace." In Ferguson and perhaps in many American communities of color, until individuals establish a means of understanding and executing their political power in a democratic fashion, violence may well be the order of the day.

Adult Educators and Black Lives Matter

This is where the challenge comes for adult educators—that of creating an informed space that can challenge students' understanding and response to the movement both engaging students and the community in critical dialogue around race (Sheared et al., 2010). Schwartz, drawing on Mills's notion of the social imagination (as cited in Schwartz, 2014), calls this *temporal space*. Temporal space is not physical but mental and emotional space where connections are made between the present and history. It is a space of intergenerational knowledge and voice where an individual's problems are understood in relation to larger social and economic contexts (Schwartz, 2014).

As learner-centered educators, we have a role in shaping the way in which students understand both social–historical perspectives and assisting our students in making sense of them within their own personal and contemporary experience. As a White adult educator, I (Joni) understand the movement and the promotion of the movement as a collaborative interracial effort against the dehumanization of another group. For the Black males and other men of color we teach, this may very well mean making sense of the Black Lives Matter movement from their own sense of identity and experience as a Black male in American society, and then examining the role and agency they may be able to play within the movement.

As Ferguson and other spaces have proven, there is a boiling of resentment and strife. The response to the continuous slaughter of unarmed Black men has sparked organic responses that are the product of a feeling within oppressed communities that the political structure is a failing one. The hope of America as a democratic institution begins to seem more like a fallacy used to oppress and suppress, while mouthing the hope of change and justice.

Again, this is where adult educators have a role. With equal engagement of our adult students, adult educators can help promote critical analysis of the movement, including classroom reading, writing, and discussion about issues of race and policing that were the initial impetus for the movement. Then, educators and students can explore local Black Lives Matter events and protests to see how adult students might participate. One adult learning community is engaging in a Theatre of the Oppressed presentation that engages both students and audience in an examination of complex issues surrounding the movement, such as gentrification, police brutality, and school trauma, that often affect adult students; developed by the students, this activism through art (LaGuardia Performing Arts Center, 2015) can provide students with a sense of agency. These plans may be localized within our own classrooms, community organizations, community colleges, churches, and adult education programs. The following section describes one community college's attempt to create this temporal space.

One Community College Engagement Initiative

During the early protests of the Black Lives Matter movement, LaGuardia Community College (LAGCC)-City University of New York responded by creating educational forums to engage and educate students around the history, contexts and rationale that precipitated the movement. LAGCC is located in New York City and serves approximately 49,000 full- and part-time students annually in both its adult and continuing education and college courses. In 2013, 71% of its students' households made $25,000 or less, 20% of LAGCC's students self-identify as Black, 42% Hispanic, 22% Asian, and 15% White (LAGCC Office of Research & Assessment, 2015).

One of the first educational forums was called *Seeking Solidarity: Lessons from Ferguson*. Created by the LAGCC Social Science Department, the forum engaged students, faculty, and staff in presentations featuring organizers and participants from Ferguson who were actively part of the movement on the streets. The second forum was a *Black Lives Matter Summit: Perception,*

Possibilities & Progress sponsored by the Black Male Empowerment Collaborative. This ongoing summit focused on four issues affecting Black males: educational inequality, mental and physical health, policing, and mass incarceration from the perspective of social activism. Approximately 300 individuals—students, adult educators, and college faculty, staff, community members, invited presenters—participated at various junctures during the daylong summit.

The majority of time was devoted to four separate and concurrent panel presentations in the morning on each issue and with the afternoon returning to the four focus groups for small and large group discussions with the goal of recommending solutions toward change at the college and community levels. A biannual return to the summit is the strategy. The remainder of this chapter explores the findings of the focus groups on these four issues.

Black Minds Matter: Education as a Civil Right. Presentations in the morning session centered around issues of unequal access to high-quality education for Blacks in poor urban neighborhoods and the impact of both gentrification and housing segregation on the quality of education. The reality is that we are now more segregated as a nation than before Brown vs. Board of Education, which then unfortunately affects resources for neighborhood schools and has resulted in poorer quality educational opportunities (access to experienced teachers, state-of-the-art technology, safe and well-maintained facilities, etc.) for Black students (Ladson-Billings, 2006). The group asserted that lack of educational equity in America is one of the greatest civil rights issues of our day.

Panelists in discussion with participants talked about projects such as the Eagle Academy (http://www.eaglebronx.org/) and other community-based adult education centers like Turning Point Brooklyn (http://www.tpbk.org/education-center.html) that are concrete alternatives to a failed public school system in poor communities of color in New York City and a response to the issue of equity. The group was very concerned about taking responsibility for change and not staying in what the group called a deficit framework. Concrete ideas about how churches, individuals, and community-based organizations can make a difference in providing mentoring, tutoring, and adult education classes were discussed by individuals who had actually created such learning forums; these ideas seemed doable and possible.

In addition, the group talked about the role of Whites in the Black Lives Matter movement, and it was noted that few Whites participated in the summit. There was concern expressed and a resolution that recruitment of White participants for future summits was crucial; otherwise there was a sense that "we are preaching to the choir." The group agreed that issues raised by the movement ought to be everyone's concern as the impact is upon the quality of life of all Americans. Solidarity was also raised as essential to the success of efforts to address one another and build a community on the campus through the movement and the Black Male Empowerment Collaborative.

New Directions for Adult and Continuing Education • DOI: 10.1002/ace

Health Matters—Mental Health and Wellness

This panel included mainly mental health professionals from the college and community as well as one student. The issues of both access to mental health counseling in communities of color and stigmas within Black communities against accessing mental health services were discussed. The panel determined that particularly for Black males the concept of seeking help has been culturally discouraged—you need to be strong and not show your feelings because that is weak, and weakness for the Black male makes you vulnerable.

The panel also discussed issues around trauma and the Black male (Van Thompson & Schwartz, 2014) and how communities of violence, particularly violence around schools and with gangs, make some Black males susceptible to traumatic experiences (Schwartz & Schwartz, 2012). This panel did not come up with concrete solutions but agreed that conversations around accessing affordable mental health services in poor communities, advocating for mental health policies that provide coverage, and dispelling stigmas about counseling were needed.

The Hood Matters—Police Brutality and Community Responsibility. This panel featured a collection of social activists, a retired police officer, and the head of security for LAGCC and was one of the most well-attended panels of the summit. The session had a dual focus. The first focus was on participants taking personal responsibility; this means being aware of certain neighborhoods and understanding potential danger in your environment, choosing good friends and associates, and being respectful of the authorities. In addition, taking personal responsibility means knowing your rights as a citizen; these steps will minimize the frequency of police stops and searches and by definition the probability of an encounter that may escalate.

The second focus of the panel was on taking action after a violation by police to your body has been committed. The panel gave attention to the sentiment of anger and frustration that is ever present after one of these incidents, but strongly pointed out that too often the anger subsides and withers down to little more than angry protest, thus allowing for a continuation of police offenses. The panel suggested community education and creation of community boards and advisory panels to both manage relations between the community and the police and work to increase the proportion of individuals who are politically active within the community, a step that would demand accountability and ensure actuation of policy. As the moderator of the panel said, "Nearly 84% of the community in Ferguson protested as a part of the Black Lives Matter' movement and other protest, and yet, 2 weeks later, less than 30% of this same community voted." He did not cite his source for these numbers, but his point was well taken. Although protest is a useful tool, it is nearly pointless and ineffective if not followed up by policy. The panel encouraged continued participation in the movement but also advocated for direct community involvement and self-efficacy, with an end goal of direct political involvement in both large federal elections, but local, specific elections that directly affect the outcomes of local issues and office holders.

Who I Am Matters: Race, Violence, and Mass Incarceration. This panel was composed of five individuals: three who are formerly incarcerated, one educator, and a student; all of whom are active in one or more of the issues being discussed by the panel: race, violence, and mass incarceration. The impetus of the session focused on engagement and direct action. First, the development of the session topic was presented by the panel with all of its complications and its implications for both the individual and society at large. The three interconnecting issues of race, violence, and mass incarceration were discussed as they intersect and affect educational opportunity and retention.

The panelists all provided information regarding current and upcoming trainings and workshops surrounding self-efficacy and "knowing your rights." These were practical doable actions. One point of consensus among the panelists was the need to rethink the issues of the day surrounding the Black Lives Matter movement but, more important, to change the way that those who are being oppressed see and treat each other (Marable & Mullings, 2009, p. 416). This point ended up being extremely important to participants—are Blacks really in solidarity? The moderator closed by explaining the movement in the context of the BMEC ("Black" Male Empowerment Cooperative) slogan: "We all we got ... We all we need." The session referred to collective oppression theory (Shelby, 2002, p. 255) explaining that the issues facing the hood are significantly related to those doing the oppression, but are forever unchanging until the problem is identified and every victim of this oppression becomes a "we/us" and not a them or they. Some feel that although the "all we need" slogan does emphasize intragroup strength, it seems to exclude the need for anyone else. It was explained that this is not the case—yes, collective solidarity is key but welcomes antiracist allies of all races, creeds, and ethnic backgrounds who share the struggle. This issue of solidarity among Blacks and antiracist Whites was key to the discussion.

Conclusion

In the introduction of this chapter, we stated that our purpose was to call *you*, the adult educator and student, to action and to further challenge all of us in how we can critically engage the Black Lives Matter movement through our work as adult educators. Our engagement in the previously described community college setting is clearly one localized ongoing attempt. This community college Black Lives Matter Summit was just a beginning, but a significant one. The design for the Black Lives Matter Summit was to develop strategies for change at the community college and in the community and for students and faculty alike to be agents of that change. A second summit is planned for this year as a follow-up. How successful participants will be in actually designing workable strategies still remains to be seen.

Although concrete movement toward change from the summit is still to be determined, what is certain is that this event did create temporal space—that dimension of learning like social imagination first defined by Mills (2000). This is the space where the Black male's personal experience and struggle with his identity as a Black man in America can intersect with larger global and national contexts, in this case the Black Lives Matter movement. The goal in creating these temporal spaces is the connection between personal worlds and the systems world (Habermas, 1989; Schwartz, 2014) and the engagement in critical, rational dialogue that leads to agency and change. This is the space of effective adult education.

What are concrete ways to create these spaces in adult education? First, in the classroom in the midst of reading, writing, and dialogue in preparation for the GED or in adult literacy classrooms as well as college settings where social justice issues can be raised. In addition, in English for speakers of other language classes, new immigrants need to understand how race in America is understood in contrast to their nations of origin. Beyond the classroom, specific events that engage both the community and adult education students can be effective: theatre of the oppressed productions that engage the Black Lives Matter movement, panels, workshops, and talks with the police and students for informed dialogue are crucial. Particularly for adult educators who work with men of color regularly, creative ways of engagement are necessary.

Clearly the lived experience of being a Black man in America and all that means from the perspective of one's own identity and the way America *names* you is in some ways at the heart of the Black Lives Matter movement. For adult educators of all races and ethnic backgrounds to be able to make room for that temporal space where Black male students can connect and understand their personal experiences with the police, with the criminal justice system, with failed schools and with their own mental health within larger sociological and historical perspectives—institutionalized racism, historical social activism, White privilege, generational trauma, global oppression—seems to be a worthwhile goal. Understanding the genesis and underlying frameworks of oppression of the Black Lives Matter movement is authentic adult education for all.

References

Alexander, M. (2010). *The new Jim Crow: Mass incarceration in the age of colorblindness.* New York: New Press.

Culp, J. (1998). To the bone: Race and white privilege. *Minnesota Law Review, 83,* 1637–1679.

DuBois, W. E. B. (1903). *The souls of black folks.* New York: Bantam Classic.

Gabrielson, R., Grochowski Jones, R., & Sagara, E. (2014). Deadly force in Black and White. ProPublica. Retrieved from http://www.propublica.org/article/deadly-force-in-black-and-white

Gorski, P. (2011). Unlearning deficit ideology and the scornful gaze: Thoughts on authenticating the class discourse in education. In R. Ahlquist, P. Gorski, & T. Montaño (Eds.),

Assault on kids: How hyper-accountability, corporatization, deficit ideology, and Ruby Payne are destroying our schools. New York: Peter Lang.

Habermas, J. (1989). *The theory of communicative action. Reason and the rationalization of society* (Vol. 1, T. McCarthy, Trans.) Boston: Beacon Press.

Johnson-Bailey, J., & Cervero, R. (1998). Power dynamics in teaching and learning practices: An examination of two adult education classrooms. *Journal of Lifelong Education*, 17(6), 289–399.

Ladson-Billings, G. (2006). From the achievement gap to the education debt: Understanding achievement in US schools. *Educational Researcher*, 35(7), 3–12.

LaGuardia Community College Office of Institutional Research and Assessment. (2015). Institutional profile: Fast facts. Retrieved from http://www.lagcc.cuny.edu/About/Fast-Facts/

LaGuardia Performing Arts Center. (2015). Perform to reform. Theatre of the oppressed. Retrieved from http://www.lpac.nyc/event/6d9019cfbb018f1722ae8c2bd59145b9

Marable, M., & Mullings, L. (2009). Malcom X and revolutionary black nationalism. In M. Marable & L. Mullings, *Let nobody turn us around: An African American anthology* (2nd ed.). New York: Rowman & Littlefield.

McIntosh, P. (1988). White privilege: Unpacking the invisible knapsack. Excerpt from *White privilege and male privilege: A personal account of coming to see correspondences through work in women's studies.* Wellesley, MA: Wellesley College Center for Research on Women.

Mills, C. W. (2000). *The sociological imagination* (40th ed.). New York: Oxford University Press.

Omi, M., & Winant, H. (1994). *Racial formation in the United States: From the 1960s to the 1990s* (2nd ed.). New York: Routledge.

Rasmussen Reports. (2015). Is equal justice the goal of Black Lives Matter? http://www.rasmussenreports.com/public_content/politics/general_politics/november_2015/is_equal_justice_the_goal_of_black_lives_matter

Ross, J. (2015, August). How Black Lives Matter moved from a hashtag to a real political force. *Washington Post.*

Schwartz, J. (2014). Classrooms of spatial justice: Counter-spaces and young men of color in a GED® program. *Adult Education Quarterly*, 64(2), 110–127.

Schwartz, P., & Schwartz, J. (Producers) (2012). *A new normal: Young men of color, trauma, and engagement in learning* [Motion picture]. New York: City University of New York. Retrieved from https://lagcc-cuny.digication.com/joni_schwartz_ph_d/Documentary

Sheared, V., Johnson-Bailey, J., Colin, S., Peterson, E., & Brookfield, S. (Eds.). (2010). *The handbook of race and adult education.* San Francisco, CA: Jossey-Bass.

Shelby, T. (2002). Foundations of Black solidarity: Collective identity or common oppression? *Ethics*, 112(2), 231–266.

Shore, S. (2001). Talking about whiteness: "Adult learning principle" and the invisible norm. In V. Sheared & P. Sissel (Eds.), *Making space: Merging theory and practice in adult education.* Westport, CT: Greenwood Publishing Group.

Smedley, A., & Smedley, B. (2005). Race as biology is fiction, racism as a social problems is real: Anthropological and historical perspectives on the social construction of race. *American Psychologist*, 60(1), 16–26.

Valentina, Z. (2015, July 19). Founders of #Black Lives Matter: Getting credit for your work matters. *Fortune Magazine.*

Van Thompson, C., & Schwartz, P. (2014). A new normal: Young men of color, trauma, and engagement in learning. In D. Rosser-Mims, J. Schwartz, B. Drayton & T. Guy (Eds.), *New Directions in Adult and Continuing Education: No. 144. Swimming upstream: Black males in adult education,* (pp.49–58). San Francisco, CA: Jossey-Bass.

BRIAN MILLER *is a recent graduate of the City University of New York and former coordinator of the Black Male Empowerment Cooperative at LaGuardia Community College.*

JONI SCHWARTZ *is an associate professor in the Humanities Department at the City University of New York, LaGuardia Community College.*

New Directions for Adult and Continuing Education • DOI: 10.1002/ace

2

This chapter focuses on the role adult educators can play in assisting Black men to overcome the challenges faced in accessing and using digital technology and acquiring appropriate skills in a digital society.

Black Men and the Digital Divide

Simone C. O. Conceição, Larry G. Martin

Led by a revolution in digital technology (such as the Internet and computers), seminal changes in information and communication knowledge and skills are imposing sweeping and enduring social, economic, and technological transformations upon an increasingly global, interconnected, and networked world. For example, a recent survey by the Pew Research Center found that 89% of American adults use the Internet (Purcell & Rainie, 2014).

Driven by the increased use of the Internet, cell phones, and other technologies, digital technology access and use have become ubiquitous in 21st-century America. The majority of adult Americans reported that their use of digital technology informed their learning needs (for products and services to buy, national and international news, and popular culture); helped them to stay updated on topics of interest to them (that is, hobbies and personal interests, health and fitness); and increased their ability to share ideas and creations with friends, family, and neighbors (Purcell & Rainie, 2014).

Access to and the ability to use social and media networks are key resources and skills needed by those seeking social and economic mobility (van Dijk, 2012; Dixon et al., 2014). Technological change driven by innovation, creativity, and the profit motive is either significantly improving the socioeconomic standing of Americans or driving a wedge, further separating different classes. The notion of a digital divide is critically important to Black men in America. Many Black men are still struggling against the tides of history as they pursue the American dream and adjust to the quickening pace of technological change.

According to Jackson et al. (2008), the term "digital divide" has historically been used to describe "the gap between those who had access to new information technology (IT) and those who did not" (p. 437). In this definition, the focus was on income and education. However, today this definition has evolved to refer to the gap in the intensity and nature of IT use rather than

NEW DIRECTIONS FOR ADULT AND CONTINUING EDUCATION, no. 150, Summer 2016 © 2016 Wiley Periodicals, Inc.
Published online in Wiley Online Library (wileyonlinelibrary.com) • DOI: 10.1002/ace.20183

mere access to it (Kvasny & Trauth, 2003; Ritzhaupt, Liu, Dawson, & Barron, 2013). This new definition signals the extent to which social and media networks, which are powerful indicators of structural inequity in the network society, have reproduced the existing social and economic inequalities between rich and poor, urban and rural, and ethnic White majority and persons of color (Dixon et al., 2014).

In a previous publication focusing on Black males and adult education, Rosser-Mims, Schwartz, Drayton, and Guy (2014) addressed the sociohistorical and embedded stereotypes that constrain the lived experiences of Black men and how these stereotypes affect their lives. Those authors also addressed the sociopolitical and cultural context of adult education and how it can influence the success of Black men in and outside the classroom. In this chapter, we consider the sociohistorical and sociopolitical issues that affect the personal and professional lives of Black men as the use of digital technology becomes omnipresent.

Many Black men still struggle to obtain a high-quality education, to acquire employment that pays a family-supporting wage, and to nurture their children and communities as fathers and role models. Their communities suffer social and economic oppression; men suffer the soul-destroying terror of violence perpetrated by Black-on-Black crime and dysfunctional social behaviors within urban communities. The majority of Black men are fully committed to live a dignified and fulfilling life. However, the digital divide is a critical challenge as these men seek to become more fully integrated into the social and economic fabric of our society. Unequal access to digital technology is equivalent to unequal access to economic participation, social interactions and networking, politics and voting, cultural engagement, spatial mobility, and institutional citizenship (van Dijk, 2012).

Digital technology access and use have evolved into one of the key basic skills (in addition to reading, writing, and math) that are necessary for full participation in our democratic society. For example, the Organisation for Economic Cooperation and Development (OECD, 2013) report shows that problem solving in technology-rich environments was identified as a key literacy skill—the ability to use digital technology, communication tools, and networks to acquire and evaluate information, communicate with others, and perform practical test. However, a dearth of research and literature clouds our understanding of how advances in digital technology affect the plight of Black men. In this chapter, we use a relational or network approach (van Dijk, 2012) to understand the digital divide between Black men and other demographic groups. Therefore, we focus on the positions of individuals and the relationships (that is, the bonds, interactions, and transactions) between them (van Dijk, 2012). Van Dijk argues that this perspective views inequality as a function of the categorical differences between groups of people, that is, Black/White, men/women, which direct attention to the relative inequality between people and their positions and resources.

New Directions for Adult and Continuing Education • DOI: 10.1002/ace

Relational or Network Approach to Digital Divide

A relational or network approach (van Dijk, 2012) suggests that the analysis of the digital divide should focus on four key points, which we present in the form of questions:

- What motivates Black men to access and use digital technology?
- How does physical and material access to digital technology differ for Black men?
- What is the level and extent of digital technology usage (time and frequency, types of applications, broadband or narrowband, active or creative) of Black men?
- What are the digital skills (such as information skills and strategic skills) of Black men?

We use available survey data, investigatory studies, and other literature to answer these questions.

Motivation to Use Digital Technology. The factors explaining motivational access are of both a social or cultural and a mental or psychological nature (van Dijk, 2012). Because digital technology is ubiquitous, people can be motivated to engage it or to avoid and distance themselves from its effects. Kvasny and Trauth (2003) found that Black men adopt three different positions.

The first group views digital technology as a form of cultural domination positioned to enslave Black men. The Internet is not seen as a portal of opportunity; it offers the same limited chances, dead-end opportunities, and disappointments that are experienced in the built world. Through self-exclusion, men in this group question the value of the Internet to the overall Black community. Rejecting technology training, they seek to carve out a space in the margins of society without the benefit of technology and label Black men engaged in digital technology as "acting White" or "doing women work" (p. 280).

A second group views engagement with digital technology as a means to assimilate and integrate within a digital society. Men in this group fear being left behind and excluded from the rich cache of resources available on the Internet; they seek to use digital technology as a means to integrate into the power structure and retain their self-esteem. For example, Black men are among the GED program participants, community and technical college students, 4-year college students, workforce development participants, employees, and workers who find the Internet and various technologies indispensable to their learning and employment efforts.

The third group views digital technology as a tool to both challenge the status quo and to wrestle power of discourse away from the dominant group. Men in this group create their own career aspirations and use digital technology in new ways for new purposes. A recent example is provided by Romiel (2014). It involves the integration of participatory politics and digital

New Directions for Adult and Continuing Education • DOI: 10.1002/ace

technology with the use of blogs or Facebook to organize the Black Lives Matter protests against the unwarranted police killings of unarmed Black men in urban centers across the country. Banks, an associate professor and director of writing, rhetoric, and digital media at the University of Kentucky, argues that technology is a mechanism for negotiating discourse through rhetorical acts focused on race, culture, and individual collective identities.

A second example of the third group involves a nefarious use of digital technology. It is drawn from a recent front-page news story in Milwaukee, Wisconsin (Diedrich, 2015). A new class of illegal drug dealer (who used stolen cars outfitted with darkly tinted windows as rolling drug houses) made innovative use of cell phone videos to capture the challenges some Black men pose to their own communities. Played in a courtroom, the 7-minute smartphone video taken by one of the Black men and posted in Facebook, featured a midday scene in urban Milwaukee where over three dozen people congregated on a dead-end street. The apparent purpose of the video was to recruit new members to a street gang. The video began with a 21-year-old Black man holding what was identified as a MAC-10 assault-style rifle. He proclaimed, "It's MAC-aroni time," as other young Black men brazenly waved guns and displayed large stacks of cash before the camera. They boasted about selling drugs and threatened to shoot at police if they appeared. Children sat on a stoop watching the drama. The video provided insight into the reckless and violent behavior responsible for over 100 deaths (many of them children and bystanders) in inner-city Milwaukee over the course of 8 months. In this case, the digital technology (cell phone video and Facebook) were used by a local street gang to send a recruiting and marketing message of plentiful access to money, drugs, and power to preteens and teenaged inner-city males.

Physical and Material Access to Digital Technology. Van Dijk (2012) and Beckles (1997) noted that physical access to personal computers and the Internet involves purchasing not only the core hardware of a computer and peripheral equipment but also modem and Internet software, Internet carrier, computer and Internet training, user support services, and materials (such as paper and ink, software, and subscriptions). Van Dijk (2012) indicated that although the hardware costs for single devices have experienced a downward trend, the number of devices purchased has trended upward. Although the physical access gap is closing, income inequalities remain important for material access (Beckles, 1997; van Dijk, 2012). Though the Internet has been characterized as a new source of democratic power for the 21st century, it could continue to be the domain of historically privileged groups and those with the financial resources to afford it. For economically challenged Black men and families, the costs of affording the Internet could place the ownership of an Internet-connected computer out of reach (Beckles, 1997).

Smith's (2014) survey results confirmed a complex demographic snapshot of technology access and use by African Americans and Whites across age, income, and education levels. Smith's survey of 6010 American adults, which included 664 African Americans, indicated that Blacks trail Whites by 7 percentage points in overall Internet use (87% of Whites and 80% of Blacks are Internet users) and by 12 percentage points in home broadband adoption (74% of Whites and 62% of Blacks have some sort of connection at home). Additionally, he found that Blacks aged 65 and over and those who have not attended college are significantly less likely to either go online or to have broadband service at home compared to Whites with a similar demographic profile (Smith, 2014). However, younger college-educated (ages 18–29) and higher income Blacks are just as likely as their White counterparts to use the Internet and to have broadband service at home. He found that 86% of young Black Americans, 88% of Black college graduates, and 91% of Blacks with an annual household income of $75,000 or more per year had adopted home broadband services. He noted that these figures are above the national average for broadband adoption and are comparable to findings for Whites of similar age, income, and education levels. Consequently, computer access and use of the Internet continue the pattern of racial and economic segregation, which fosters an "information elite" that has full access of the most powerful technology.

Blacks, Whites, and Hispanics have similar rates of smartphone ownership (Anderson, 2015); and Blacks and Whites are equally likely to own a cell phone or smartphone (Smith, 2014). However, persons of color tend to rely more heavily on their phones for Internet access (Anderson, 2015). About 92% of Black adults own cell phones and 56% own smartphones. Among Black adults aged 65 and over, 77% own cell phones. In total, 72% of all Black adults and 98% of those between the ages of 18 and 29 have either a broadband connection or a smartphone (Smith, 2014). About 13% of Hispanics and 12% of Blacks are smartphone dependent; they do not have a broadband connection at home, and they have few options for going online other than their cell phones (Anderson, 2015).

In contrast, only about 4% of White smartphone owners rely heavily on their cell phones for online access. Blacks rely more heavily on smartphones than Whites for information about health, online banking, real estate, government services, educational content, and job applications (Anderson, 2015). More than half (55%) of Black smartphone owners reported using their phones in the past year to find job information compared to about one-third (37%) of Whites. Blacks are more than twice as likely as Whites to submit a job application by smartphone (Anderson, 2015). About 32% of Blacks have used their mobile device to take an online class or search for educational content in the past year, compared to 26% of Whites (Anderson, 2015).

Level and Extent of Digital Technology Usage. The concepts of "level" and "extent" of digital technology usage are defined by several parameters: the usage time and frequency of applications, number and diversity of usage applications, broadband or narrowband use, and more or less active or creative use of technology (van Dijk, 2012). When examining technology use, it is important to note not only the length of time and frequency of use but for what purposes. For example, people with low levels of education tend to use popular applications (such as chatting, online gaming, receiving audiovisual programs, social media networking, and shopping), which require a relatively long usage time (van Dijk, 2012).

Although research documents a dramatic reduction in race differences in Internet use (Jackson et al., 2008), Internet use differs greatly between Black American adults and any other racial group. Black Americans are more likely to use the Internet to search for religious or spiritual information and they are less likely to use it for communication (Jackson et al., 2008). The gender divide among all races and ethnicities in the nature of Internet use also persists. Men tend to be more frequent and intense users of the Internet than women (Dixon et al., 2014). Adult females are more likely to use the Internet's communication tools, whereas males are more likely to use it for information, entertainment (such as playing video games), and commerce (Jackson et al., 2008). However, in their research on technology usage among 172 African American and 343 Caucasian American students from 20 middle schools, Jackson et al. (2008) found that Black males tended to spend less time using computers and that they tended to use both computers and the Internet less often than any other demographic group. Black males were the least likely to surf the Web, to buy something online, to search the Internet for school assignments or a hobby, or to use a search engine (Jackson et al., 2008). However, these young Black males in Jackson et al.'s study played video games as much as did young Caucasian American males and more than the females of any race. The researchers pointed out that video game playing is the only digital technology use linked to poorer academic performance. In contrast, Black females led other demographics in Internet use; they used the Internet more than any other group in text messaging, using the cell phone, downloading music files, and searching the Internet for information regarding a variety of topics, including physical and mental health and well-being.

Research indicated that Black adult Internet users access a variety of sites. About 96% of those aged 18–29 use a social networking site (Smith, 2014). A total of 71% of online adults use Facebook; however, among Blacks, in 2014 that percentage dropped to 67%, but it was 71% for urban adults (Duggan, Ellison, Lampe, Lenhart, & Madden, 2015). Facebook "friends" included family members other than parents or children, current friends, past friends from high school or college, work colleagues, parents, children, neighbors, and people they never met (Duggan et al., 2015).

About 23% of online adults use Twitter. It is particularly popular among those under 50 and the college educated (Duggan et al., 2015). Twitter is also the most popular social networking site among Blacks. About 22% of online Blacks are Twitter users compared to 16% of whites (Smith, 2014). Twenty-six percent of online adults use Instagram, and Blacks (38% in 2014) and those who live in urban or suburban environments are more likely than Whites (21% in 2014) to be on this platform (Duggan et al., 2015). Pinterest is popular among younger Internet users, with 28% of online adults, but Blacks (12% of users in 2014) do not have a strong presence on the site. Lastly, 28% of adult

Internet users (and 28% of Black online adults) use LinkedIn. This site tends to be particularly popular among college graduates, those in higher income households, and people who are employed (Duggan et al., 2015).

Digital Skills. Information and strategic digital skill sets refer to the capacity to work with hardware and software: the ability to search, select, and process information in computer network services. Strategic skills are the capacities to use computer and network services as the means for particular goals and for the general goal of improving one's position in society (van Dijk, 2012).

Since the 1970s, the U.S. economy has been shifting away from routine manual, nonroutine manual, and routine cognitive tasks and toward more nonroutine analytic and interpersonal tasks that require higher skills (Pawlowski, 2015). Digital technologies now play a central role in globalization of markets by increasing the speed of communication and reducing costs. Digital technologies accelerate the flow of goods, capital, people, and information across borders; they affect jobs and demand different job skills. Globalization has also increased outsourcing of production, which relocates low-skilled jobs to low-wage and low-cost locations in less-developed countries (OECD, 2013).

The use of information and communications technologies in the workplace has changed the types and levels of skills needed for workers. Economic trends indicate that employment in services and high-skilled occupations are growing (OECD, 2013). Manufacturing jobs are declining and are being offset by a growing number of service-sector jobs in finance, real estate, insurance, and business services. Levy and Murnane (2006) found that skills associated with the transmission and interpretation of information, communication, and expert thinking are essential for adult learners in the 21st century. These skills require higher levels of literacy and mathematical ability as well as access to and use of digital technology. The majority of the jobs associated with these skills are highly dependent on the use of computers.

Both the increase in high-skilled jobs and increasing globalization and relocation of low-skilled jobs negatively affect the employment prospects of Black men. Data from the Program for International Assessment of Adult Competencies (PIAAC) indicated that a greater percentage of U.S. adults working in unskilled and semiskilled occupations are low performers in literacy compared to peers across participating countries. Also, the same data showed that among employed U.S. adults, those who have low literacy skills are more likely to be Black or Hispanic (Pawlowski, 2015).

Many of the government, social, and economic services (such as Social Security services, banking and finance, library, college and employment applications and services) that benefit American citizens require Internet service and the ability to navigate complex websites. Low-income individuals have less access to all these services (Pilling & Boeltzig, 2007). These barriers not only prevent the increase of access and use by Black men, but they also place them at a disadvantage to receive critical services and to be active members of society.

Our analysis of the research and literature suggests that the digital divide for Black men parallels access and use along the lines of individual and family affluence. For lower income Black men, the digital divide starts in grade school, when disparities of access and use of digital technologies are abundant and continue until individuals are of working age and need technological skills to obtain employment in a globalized society. Lower income Black men struggle to find and use various forms of digital technology in their homes, schools, and places of employment.

Adult Education's Role in Helping Black Men Succeed

Black Americans who have middle-class educations and incomes do not experience the access issues that affect those who are resource poor. Adult education can play an important role in helping low-income Black men succeed in their workplaces, communities, and personal lives. Different educational interventions can assist learners to gain access to and use digital technology as a means to seek social–cultural change, obtain employment, advance in a job/career, and access available assistance.

Many Black men face a multitude of challenges to improving their levels of digital technology proficiency. First, a widespread perception is that Black men are users of technology but not creators of it. Statistics tracking the college participation and success of Black male students in science, technology, engineering, and mathematics (STEM) majors and IT-related careers seem to justify this perspective. For example, the proportion of Black men to White men at the PhD level indicates how well the country is preparing them to reach the pinnacle of technology innovation and engagement. This number more than doubled between 1992 and 2012; however, the actual amount was minimal, an increase from only 1% to 2% of all STEM degrees (Patton, 2014). In 1992, Black men earned 139 of the 11,485 STEM doctorates awarded, and in 2012, they earned 334 of 16,545 STEM doctorates (Patton, 2014).

In an effort to improve such low numbers, DiSalvo et al. (2009) designed a research intervention, Glitch Game Testers, involving resource-poor 15-year-old Black teenagers in Atlanta. The researchers designed the intervention around a technological strength of Black males—passion for video games. Black males are the most prolific users of digital games, but they are virtually absent in the development and creation of the games. The researchers involved the teenagers in a project that paid them to test the efficacy of video games for an established game producer. Participants were strongly motivated; they tended to arrive 30 minutes early to play games or work on programming projects. Eleven of 12 students decided to focus on computer science in college after participating in this intervention (DiSalvo et al., 2009).

Second, interventions should focus on another strength of Black men. Many use smartphones as a primary means to connect to the Internet for a wide variety of social and educational programs and services. Educational and service providers should design their websites to be easily navigated via the use of cell phones.

Third, educational interventions can be offered in neighborhood associations, nongovernmental organizations, public libraries, community or technical colleges, and employment settings. Neighborhood and nonprofit organizations can provide short courses on technological skills. Libraries can continue to provide access to computers and computer training. Technical or community colleges can increase their efforts to prepare Black men for the GED test that is now offered using digital technology.

Pilling and Boeltzig (2007) identified strategies for increasing access and use of Internet by low-income individuals. For individuals who lack awareness of the benefits of the Internet and e-government, they suggested designing easy-to-use websites covering information and including links to local government and other websites. Libraries can include this type of information through Internet training classes or formal training on e-government websites (for example, training would explain what services are offered and how they can be accessed and navigated). Provide home computers and Internet connections and provide training and support at home for isolated or homebound people who cannot afford technology. Training could be either informal one-to-one or group teaching. Participants would be encouraged to make connections with others and to get engaged in communal efforts.

Fourth, community-based organizations can get Black men involved in group-based or self-directed learning to enhance basic knowledge and technology skills. A community-improvement plan would be an effective method of including those who view digital technology as a form of cultural domination and reject its access and use. It is important to emphasize the development of math skills among young Black males in K–12 and teach math differently so that they create an appreciation for learning and mastering math concepts early in their academic careers. As young adults, they should be engaged with incubators and innovative spaces for entrepreneurial ideas in inner cities. For the broader community of Black males, community-based organizations should offer classes on how to purchase appropriate technology and where to use technology without having to purchase home Internet and additional courses on computer coding and app creation. Examples of community-based groups that can help Black men become involved include "My Brother's Keeper" (http://mbk.ed.gov/), "100 Black Men of America" (http://www.100blackmen.org/mentoring.aspx), "Black Professional Men" (http://www.blackprofessionalmen.org/community-based-programs/), and "Fathers Making Progress." By participating in community-based groups and initiatives, Black men can envision the limitless possibilities that digital technology can offer for growth and development of their personal knowledge and skills. Their digital knowledge and skills can contribute to their communities, families, and workplaces through activism, social networking, and the digital success of their family members.

Future of Digital Technology in Society

The 21st-century technological revolution has ushered in change on a scale and pace never before seen in human history. The next great leap in digital technology will likely be in the realm of the Internet of Things—a global, immersive, invisible, ambient, networked computing environment built by the continued proliferation of smart sensors, cameras, software, databases, and massive data centers in a world-spanning information fabric (Anderson & Rainie, 2015). Portable, wearable, and implantable technologies will likely disrupt established 20th-century business models (most notably, finance, entertainment, publishing, and education). Technology will be ubiquitously found on our bodies, in our homes, and communities; it will be inserted into our goods and services and transplanted into our natural environments (Anderson & Rainie, 2015). Technology will continue to evolve and carries the potential to facilitate solutions to the digital divide.

With appropriate and timely interventions, digital gaming, cell phones, portable technology, and library computers can connect Black men to the world of digital technologies, employment opportunities, and community engagement.

References

Anderson, M. (2015, April 1). 6 facts about Americans and their smartphones. *Pew Research Center Fact Tank: News in the Numbers.* Retrieved from http://www. pewresearch.org/fact-tank/2015/04/01/6-facts-about-americans-and-their-smartphones/ http://www.pewresearch.org/fact-tank/2015/04/01/6-facts-about-americans-and-their-smartphones/

Anderson, J., & Rainie, L. (2015). *The Internet of things will thrive by 2025* (Research Report No. 202.419.4500). Retrieved from http://www.pewinternet.org/2014/ 05/14/internet-of-things/http://www.pewinternet.org/2014/05/14/internet-of-things/

Beckles, C. (1997). Black struggles in cyberspace: Cyber-segregation and cyber-Nazis. *Western Journal of Black Studies, 21*(1), 12–19.

Diedrich, J. (2015, August 29). Brazen video shows guns, threats: Man sentenced to 19 years on drug-gun charges. *Milwaukee Journal Sentinel,* pp. 1, 4A.

DiSalvo, B., Guzdial, M., Mcklin, T., Meadows, C., Perry, K., Steward, C., et al. (2009). Glitch game testers: African American men breaking open the console. *Proceedings of the 2009 DiGRA International Conference: Breaking new ground: Innovation in games, play, practice and theory.* Retrieved from http://homes.lmc.gatech.edu/ ~cpearce3/DiGRA09/Friday%204%20September/114%20Glitch%20Game%20Testers. pdf

Dixon, L. J., Correa, T., Straubhaar, J., Covarrubias, L., Graber, D., Spence, J., et al. (2014). Gendered space: The digital divide between male and female users in Internet public access sites. *Journal of Computer-Mediated Communication, 19*(4), 991–1009.

Duggan, M., Ellison, N. B., Lampe, C., Lenhart, A., & Madden, M. (2015). *Social media update 2014: While Facebook remains the most popular site, other platforms see higher rates of growth* (Research Report No. 202.419.4372). Retrieved from http://www. pewinternet.org/2015/01/09/social-media-update-2014/http://www.pewinternet.org/ 2015/01/09/social-media-update-2014/

Jackson, L. A., Zhao, Y., Kolenic, A., III, Fitzgerald, H. E., Harold, R., & Von Eye, A. (2008). Race, gender, and information technology use: The new digital divide. *CyberPsychology & Behavior, 11*(4), 437–442.

Kvasny, L., & Trauth, E. M. (2003). The digital divide at work and home: The discourse about power and underrepresented groups in the information society. In E. H. Wynn, E. Whitley, M. Myers, & J. DeGross (Eds.), *Global and organizational discourse about information technology* (pp. 273–291). New York: Springer US.

Levy, F., & Murnane, R. J. (2006). Why the changing American economy calls for twenty-first century learning: Answers to educators' questions. *New Directions for Youth Development: No. 110. The case for twenty-first century learning* (pp. 53–62). San Francisco, CA: Jossey-Bass. doi: 10.1002/yd.167

Organisation for Economic Cooperation and Development. (2013). *OECD skills outlook 2013: First results from the Survey of Adult Skills.* Paris: OECD Publishing. Retrieved from http://dx.doi.org/10.1787/9789264204256-en

Patton, S. (2014, October 27). Black man in the lab: Why do so few black men earn STEM degrees? The reasons, and the remedies, go beyond numbers. *Chronicle of Higher Education.* Retrieved from http://chronicle.com/article/article-content/149565/http://chronicle.com/article/article-content/149565/

Pawlowski, E. (2015). Low skilled workforce in the U.S.: Key findings from the Program for International Assessment of Adult Competency (PIAAC). In *Proceedings of the Adult Education Research Conference*, Manhattan, KS (pp. 292–296).

Pilling, D., & Boeltzig, H. (2007). Moving toward e-government: Effective strategies for increasing access and use of the Internet among non-Internet users in the U.S. and U.K. *Proceedings of the 8th Annual International Digital Government Research Conference*, 35–46. doi: 10.1145/1248460.1248467

Purcell, K., & Rainie, L. (2014). *Americans feel better informed thanks to the Internet.* (Research Report No. 202.419.4372). Retrieved from http://www.pewinternet.org/2014/12/08/better-informed/

Ritzhaupt, A. D., Liu, F., Dawson, K., & Barron, A. E. (2013). Differences in student information and communication technology literacy based on socio-economic status, ethnicity, and gender: Evidence of a digital divide in Florida schools. *Journal of Research on Technology in Education, 45*(4), 291–307.

Romiel, K. (2014, September 11). CSCRE discusses the use of social media as a gateway to activism. *The Ithacan.* Retrieved from http://theithacan.org/news/cscre-discusses-social-media-and-technological-media-as-gateways-to-activism/

Rosser-Mims, D., Schwartz, J., Drayton, B., & Guy, T. C. (Eds.). (2014). *New Directions for Adult and Continuing Education: No. 144. Swimming upstream: Black males in adult education.* San Francisco, CA: Jossey-Bass.

Smith, A. (2014). *African Americans and technology use: A demographic portrait* (Research Report No. 202.419.4500). Retrieved from http://pewinternet.org/Reports/2014/African-American-Tech-Use.aspx http:///h

van Dijk, J. A. G. M. (2012). The evolution of the digital divide: The digital divide turns to inequality of skills and usage. In J. Bus et al. (Eds.), *Digital enlightenment yearbook 2012* (pp. 57–75). doi: 10.3233/978-1-61499-057-4-57

SIMONE C. O. CONCEIÇÃO is a professor of adult and continuing education leadership in the School of Education at the University of Wisconsin–Milwaukee.

LARRY G. MARTIN is a professor emeritus of adult and continuing education leadership in the School of Education at the University of Wisconsin–Milwaukee.

3

The chapter captures the tensions around the research and "common wisdom" that college is an imperative for all young Black males.

Self-Directed Learning and Not Choosing College: A Counterstory

Richard Osborne, Joni Schwartz

A common narrative in America and in many Black communities is that young men of color should choose college at any cost as a way of escaping poverty and moving on with their lives. And although much research does support this narrative, this chapter aims to problematize and muddy the waters by offering a counternarrative. From two embedded frameworks, self-directed learning and critical race theory, coauthors Richard and Joni dialogue around Richard's choice "to not choose college." Richard is the insider; his experience and informed perspectives are the counterstory. Joni is the engaged outsider, a college professor. This may be a false dichotomy but does appropriately position the authors, we think, by centering on Richard's story and privileging Richard's voice. Through this dialogue, the authors have attempted to highlight not only the challenges that Black men face but also the factors that influence their decisions about choosing or not choosing college.

Self-Directed Learning and Critical Race Theory

Self-directed learning is a core adult learning theory (Houle, 1961; Knowles, 1975; Merriam, 2001; Tough, 1971) based predominantly upon the individual learner and her maturing ability to reflect upon, set goals for, make decisions in regard to, and take responsibility for her own learning over time. As a core theory, it has been criticized for ignoring the context of learning, particularly the social and political forces (Brookfield, 1993; Collins, 1996; Merriam, 2001) that position an individual's learning trajectory in very powerful and sometimes oppressive learning contexts that then inform an individual learner's choices and educational directions (Andruske, 2000).

Contrastingly, critical race theory (CRT) looks at larger contexts; as applied to adult education, the theory maintains that racism is an ever-present component of the American educational experience and that through

NEW DIRECTIONS FOR ADULT AND CONTINUING EDUCATION, no. 150, Summer 2016 © 2016 Wiley Periodicals, Inc.
Published online in Wiley Online Library (wileyonlinelibrary.com) • DOI: 10.1002/ace.20184

interest convergence Whites benefit from an institutionalized racist educational structure. CRT further maintains that differential racialized stereotypes affect different minority groups at different times to satisfy economic interests. The voices of people of color are privileged in CRT and form indispensable narratives as part of their racial identities which are not shared by Whites in America (Closson, 2010; Delgado & Stefancic, 2001; Ianinska, Wright, & Rocco, 2003; Ladson-Billings, 1999). It is within these two contrasting and embedded frameworks, self-directed learning and CRT, that the following dialogue is situated.

A Counterstory

JONI: So, Rich, let me ask you the question "Why did you not go to college, you were well able, academically prepared—what is your story?"

RICHARD: At my career level it's a fair question. It's an expected question. But I have also learned that it's a loaded question. I've sat across from well-pedigreed executives and business people and my response to this question, although rehearsed and carefully tailored, is one hundred percent true. It goes something like this. "Under different circumstances, sure, I would have loved to go to college and earn a degree. Instead, I went to work. At some points I had the time for college, at other points I had the money, but I never had both time and money at the same juncture. Sometimes I think about higher education as something that I missed out on. But if given the choice, I wouldn't trade 4 years of college for years of experience. Not in a million years."

JONI: In response, let me say that I did not mean to ask a "loaded question." But I will say, as your godmother and a college professor, I have in the past been concerned about your choice not to attend college. I am not concerned anymore because of what you have been able to achieve without college, and you are only in your late 20s. Would you tell me about your current work and recent job accomplishments?

RICH: Currently I am co-owner of a new enterprise that contracts out construction and remodeling jobs throughout New York City. After a number of years of being in supervisory and construction and maintenance management positions for large hotels and schools, I decided I wanted to be my own boss. As a start-up company, we have more than enough work; I work 7 days a week, long hours, but am growing a lucrative business with a growing number of employees. And I do this all while my wife and I raise two baby boys.

JONI: Despite your financial and professional success, Rich, I know you are not ignorant of the prevailing wisdom and research that indicate that not choosing college can have long-term financial consequences. According to a recent Pew Research Center report, college graduates as a whole over their lifetimes will earn more than half a million dollars more than high school graduates, even if the cost of college itself is factored in (Taylor et al., 2011). In addition, according to the U.S. Department of Education's National Center for Education Statistics (Kena, Aud, & Johnson, 2014), the unemployment rate for 16- to 24-year-old high school graduates with no college was 18.9% in 2013, as compared to 8.3% for college graduates of the same age. For 25- to 34-year-old full-time employees, college graduates earn 50% more than those who have not attended college. What do you say to all these statistics?

RICH: I am not sure this is the whole context, especially for Black students. First of all, it's immoral to expect teenagers to make long-term decisions that will force them to enter adulthood carrying a mountain of debt. I have observed that some graduates with a bachelor's degree still don't have a sense of what they want to do or the ability to find a well-paying job. They know that they have 6 months before they have to start paying their loans back; it's much more attractive to stay in school. This allows these students another 2 or 3 years to defer loan payments while they rack up another fifteen thousand in debt. The expectation is that having a master's degree will make them more employable. In reality, these are now adults in their mid-20s with no work experience. Jobs that require a master's degree but no experience are few and far between, and there are far too many college graduates fighting for those precious few opportunities in their chosen field.

Over 260,000 Americans with college or professional degrees are earning at or below the federal minimum wage (U.S. Department of Labor, 2015). Too many college grads are struggling to pay their student loans, so they are delaying adulthood (Kmec & Furstenberg, 2002), and entering the workforce 5–10 years later than they should have. Forget about saving or investing. Forget about marriage or home ownership.

It feels like a racket. It's way too easy to receive a student loan. An 18-year-old can have a check in his hands without understanding what the terms are. About 65% of high-debt student loan borrowers were surprised by or misunderstood aspects of their loans or the borrowing process (Whitsett, 2012).

As easy as student loan debt is to accumulate, it is virtually impossible to get rid of. Private citizens can declare bankruptcy to absolve mortgage, credit card, or gambling debt. Corporations can file for bankruptcy to insulate from litigation, but student loan debt is forever. Student loans are wonderful in that they allow people with limited means the opportunity to pursue higher education. However, the issue is whether that degree gives them the earning power to pay the loan back and be active participants in the economy.

JONI: Ok, I understand the argument of return on investment and borrowing and debt—and I do not totally disagree, but can we backtrack a minute? I guess I would like to know what about your past schooling experience additionally informs your strong feelings around not choosing college. Any discussion of choice about college and low academic preparation can be had only within the understanding that many urban Black males have unequal access to good primary and secondary education (Noguera & Boykin, 2011; Noguera, Ayers, Ladson-Billings, & Stovall, 2008). I don't need to remind you that this reality, coupled with racist policing practices and the American phenomenon of mass incarceration of Black males, creates a system that ill-prepares and disturbs many young men of color facing college choices (Alexander, 2010; Holzman, 2014). It is within this larger context that individual Black males have to choose. Beyond academic preparation, issues around physical and emotional safety and schools that again ill prepare Black males for even wanting to attend college should not be underestimated (Schwartz, 2014). But this is not your story. Rich, I know that you were well prepared academically for college—and still made this choice. Can you speak to this?

RICH: In my urban elementary school, each grade had five classes. One special education, one primary Spanish speakers (ESL), one less than average, one average, and one gifted class. There was no confusion. Everyone knew exactly which class they were in. Just as important, they knew what class the other kids were in. I was in the gifted class; however, it was more often referred to as "the White class," and for good reason. Now, not all the kids in the gifted class were White, but all the White kids were in the gifted class. All of them.

I was very frustrated by school. I determined early that it was mostly a scam, a way to keep kids occupied during the day so that their parents could contribute to the economy. I was frustrated by the reset button every year. September meant learning about Plymouth and Columbus—aka the beginning of time. Every February, it was Frederick Douglass, Martin Luther King, and Rosa Parks. I went to a good school in a good district, so we had music and art class; but they were repetitive, uninspired, and regimented.

It wasn't long before I was disinterested and disengaged. I learned that I only had to operate my brain at about 20% in order to skate by. And I was in the gifted class! I can articulate now what I felt then. Alone. In a class full of kids, I felt alone. I couldn't count on anyone or any existing system to prepare me for life or work or anything, really. I had to do it myself.

I got in trouble. Often. Regularly. Notes and calls home were at least a weekly occurrence, then long talks with the guidance counselor. I would be sequestered to a solitary desk abutting the teacher's desk to prevent me from distracting the other students. I remember being sent to the principal's office for getting into an argument with the music teacher after asking why we were studying the Baroque period again, same as last year and the year before. "Why can't we learn about jazz?" I demanded.

In art class we made cards for Mother's Day. I designed a beautiful card. A pastoral floral scene under a tree on the cover and a poem inside:

Roses are Red
And some are pink
You may be mean sometimes
But at least you don't stink

The art teacher was not amused. "If my daughter wrote this to me, she'd be in her room for a long time." To this day I stand by my response: "What business is it of yours what I write to my Mother?"

I wasn't well liked by my teachers. A problem to be solved. A wasted potential. Defiant. When words fail, defiant is always a safe way to describe me and other Black males. Admittedly and proudly, I have never been satisfied to simply swallow what I've been given or to follow a prescribed agenda. That's why the idea of college, at least the way it is usually framed, is so unattractive to me.

JONI: But learning is anything but unattractive to you. You are among the most self-directed learners I know. I consider myself a lifelong, self-directed learner as well. For us, the rise of the Internet and the new plethora of MOOCs (massive open online courses), free online courses offered by both universities and other educational organizations (Coursera, Instreamia, Duolingo, Saylor.org., YouTube, social media, etc.), not available a decade ago (Holford, Jarvis, Milana, Waller, & Webb, 2014), is a gold mine. Rich, tell me more about your learning.

RICH: I love learning. I do it all the time, as much as I can. I never feel like I've arrived. I'm constantly desirous to develop a different part of my brain and grow more as a person. There has never been a better time to be a self-directed learner. Years ago, if you wanted to learn a language, you had to take a night class or buy a book. Now I just reach into my pocket and download a free app, and I'm conjugating in minutes. I want to learn about bookbinding. I search the web, watch videos, follow blogs, order supplies, and I can start binding books the following afternoon. We live in a wondrous and magical time where anything we could ever want to know is easily accessible.

In the 90s dot com era, the Internet was used to democratize media. Although most people used Napster and LimeWire to download music and movies and a lot of pornography, I saw it as a window to another world. I used it to download books. A few keystrokes and I downloaded *The Communist Manifesto*. It took about 3 seconds. After slogging through that, I moved on to Milton Friedman. I started to learn about all the stuff I didn't know. I felt ignorant, which sucked, but I also felt free. I could study what I wanted on my time, at my pace. Learning became something that I did because I loved it, not because it would make me an elitist or grant me more earning power. This ability to be a lifelong learner now serves me well in the marketplace.

JONI: Yes, I agree. The ability to self-direct learning has served me well in making career changes throughout my life from public school teaching, to community organizing, to program development, management and administration, college teaching, research, and writing. Rich, explain more about your self-directed learning and the marketplace.

RICH: On any given day in a previous job (before my own business), I may be negotiating contracts, brainstorming marketing strategies, recommending menu items to the chef, developing budgets, tasting new cocktails, picking out floral arrangements—all before lunch. And if there's something I need to know more about, I have the experience and the discipline to learn it myself and apply that knowledge immediately. This makes me an extremely valuable employee because it's hard to find one person who can support as many roles as I can. I seldom have a dull day at work and every day is an adventure. I wake up knowing that I am going to have problems thrown at me, but I always feel equipped because I've always made it a priority to learn as much as I could, not just enough to enable me to pass a test or make a grade. Learning is my lifestyle, so solving problems is part of who I am, not something I do for money.

Several of my friends have multiple master's degrees. I've watched them work hard, complain, and accumulate tens and hundreds of thousands of dollars worth of student loan debt, only to come out with no conception of what to do next. They've spent 20 years in school, and they don't know how to do anything else.

Among my friends, I've always been the most financially stable. In high school I rushed to work after school to get as many hours in as possible, to learn as much and be as valuable as I could. Working with adults who were 10, 20, even 30 years my senior, I developed a taste for coffee. This proved very convenient since my high school friends worked at the local Dunkin' Donuts and a nearby Starbucks. I'd head over on a break order a latte, tip them, and sit in the corner with my laptop.

When I was 19, my friends worked at bookstores and went to college. I was working at a private college as an assistant facilities manager with a staff of 12 and business cards. I eventually hired an assistant, a father of two with master's degrees in information technology. I was 23 before I had a staff member who was younger than me.

When I was 25, I was representing my employer, a multinational corporation, at property operations meetings at a legendary New York City hotel while running multiple and concurrent multimillion-dollar renovations, operating a handful of restaurants, luxury retail stores, and event spaces.

I've always been the youngest, darkest and least educated person in executive meetings. But by listening, observing, and making learning a lifestyle, rather than a certificate or diploma; I have taught myself how to contribute to these meetings in what I think is a cogent, thoughtful way while speaking from a variety of specialties. I speak the language of finance when necessary after years of budgetary analysis, development, and management. Dealing with insurance claims and construction litigation taught me to think and speak in legal terms, and working with ownership taught me the jargon of the executives. But since I started from the absolute bottom by cleaning makeshift bathrooms on construction sites, I can still relate to frontline employees, janitors, plumbers, and technicians. For that reason, I'm extremely effective as an employee, as a manager, and as a director. This is what gives me value in the job market. Frequently, these kinds of flexible, interpersonal, and practical skills are not taught in a university (Freeman, 2013), but can come by being a lifelong learner. My experience allows me to change industries while building a broad and diverse skill set.

JONI: Now, beyond self-directed and lifelong learning—I think the audience who reads this chapter is going to say "Rich is an anomaly. We cannot apply his experience to other Black males." And, in fact, they might say that not choosing college flies in the face of the research and is just plain dangerous. What would you say to these arguments? To which I am not totally unsympathetic, by the way.

RICH: Higher education is a lucrative business that in part makes money by convincing people to take on debt and put their lives on hold, thereby delaying job entry because we have too many applicants and not enough jobs. A bachelor's degree is a way to portray one candidate as more valuable than another. It's not necessarily a complete portrait.

In addition to some of the obstacles you mentioned, Joni, working for the bachelor's degree isn't always an option, and it is often just more difficult for Blacks to obtain that degree. Precollege, when privileged students are taking high school AP courses, touring universities, and racking up extracurricular activities, many Black students are struggling with issues of emergent adulthood: caring for siblings and working to help make ends meet (Kmec & Furstenberg, 2002). AP courses generally aren't available in their schools. Neither are after-school, music and art programs. The best and most experienced teachers flock to the suburbs, while overworked guidance counselors spend most of their time trying to get kids to graduate on time and helping with college applications, which many times end up a pipe dream (Holzman, 2012)

For these reasons and others, college is largely an extension of privilege. That privilege has strong, deep roots in our country and fights tooth and nail to maintain its status. Blacks in America and around the world have a long and storied history of being undervalued. Many poor and working class families have struggled to pull themselves out of poverty for decades and for generations, only to find themselves the first victims of dips in the economy. Black unemployment is typically twice as high as White unemployment (U.S. Department of Labor, 2015).

During the recent recession, the entire country was feeling the sting of unemployment and underemployment. Cries to dismantle social equity programs were voiced anew. The optics of financial behemoths (traditionally predominantly White institutions) crumbling along with the election of the nation's first African American president seemed to communicate that the days of White privilege and Black disadvantage were over. But of course, that's nonsense.

In an unequal society, the advantaged group is always the last to know that a disaster is coming. In America, Blacks act as the canaries in the coal mine. Minorities always feel the effects of a declining economy before it hits main street. They're the first to see a reduction in hours, and layoffs, and the last to get back into the black after a recovery (Hout & Cumberworth, 2012).

JONI: Your arguments sound to me as if you are saying that college is an extension of White privilege and you are almost advocating for the concept of deschooling of America (Illich, 1973). You know, I frequently tell all of my college students, most of whom are students of color, that they "must stay in college"; that, in fact, "college is a way out" of marginalized situations and will ultimately be of benefit to them and their families. Am I wrong to say this, especially as I am positioned from privilege?

RICH: Many of my friends and acquaintances have been told, "You have to go to college." This sentiment is especially stressed in the Black community. My big qualm with this notion is that it has taken an almost superstitious tone vis-à-vis "If you don't want to be poor, go to college." The subtext easily implied is " . . . because you're worthless without a degree."

The most damaging of the prevailing myths is that America is a postracial society. This loaded, pervasive lie is at the heart of many socioeconomic issues that affect African Americans. See, if racism is over, then there's no reason Black achievement shouldn't mirror White achievement. Since it doesn't, there must be something about Black people that makes them inherently worse off. Telling Black kids that a college degree is all they need to level the playing field is patently false. Expecting the same level of achievement from Blacks as Whites is unfair. Advising Black students the same way we advise White students is a recipe for failure, bitterness, disillusionment, anger, and disengagement.

JONI: It seems to me that you are making the case for self-directed and lifelong learning and its crucial importance for all adults—but, in the context of this chapter, you apply those theories to Black males. This is not anticollege. Unquestionably, for a number of Black males, college is the appropriate choice. But you are calling into question the belief that enshrines the university system as a "magic bullet." Would you agree? The last word is yours.

RICH: Black students need to be taught to never give control of their education to someone else. However, many Black males do need to look outside the classroom for opportunities to pick up a new skill. They need to be told that they have to work smarter and harder than the privileged in order to achieve a similar level of success. They need to start gaining experience early; the value of experience cannot be underestimated. They need to be taught that they are capable of succeeding and achieving social mobility, even without following the standard format. They will be more successful if they make lifelong learning a priority, a lifestyle, not just something they do as a shortcut to a good job.

References

Alexander, M. (2010). *The new Jim Crow: Mass incarceration in the age of colorblindness*. New York: New Press.

Andruske, C. L. (2000, January). *Self-directed learning as a political act: Learning projects of women on welfare*. Paper presented at the meeting of the 41st Annual Adult Education Research Conference, Vancouver, British Columbia.

Brookfield, S. (1993). Self-directed learning, political clarity, and the critical practice of adult education. *Adult Education Quarterly*, 43(4), 227–242. doi:10.1177/0741713693043004002

Closson, R. B. (2010). Critical race theory and adult education. *Adult Education Quarterly*, 60(3), 261–283. doi:10.1177/0741713609358445

Collins, M. (1996). On contemporary practice and research: Self-directed learning to critical theory. In R. Edwards, A. Hanson, & P. Raggatt (Eds.), *Boundaries of adult learning: Adult learners, education and training*. New York: Routledge.

Delgado, R., & Stefancic, J. (2001). *Critical race theory: An introduction*. New York: New York University Press.

Freeman, K. W. (2013, October, 14). Why aren't companies getting graduates with the skills they need? *Wall Street Journal*. Retrieved from http://www.wsj.com/articles/SB10001424052702304561004579135253438812772

Holford, J., Jarvis, P., Milana, M., Waller, R., & Webb, S. (2014). The MOOC phenomenon: Toward lifelong education for all? *International Journal of Lifelong Education, 33*(5), 569–572. doi:10.1080/02601370.2014.961245

Holzman, M. (2012). *The urgency of now*. Cambridge, MA: Schott Foundation for Public Education.

Holzman, M. (2014). *The chains of black America: The hammer of the police, the anvil of the schools*. Briarcliff Manor, NY: Chelmsford Press.

Houle, C.O. (1961). *The inquiring mind*. Madison: University of Wisconsin Press.

Hout, M., & Cumberworth, E. (2012, October). *The labor force and the great recession*. Stanford, CA: Russell Sage Foundation and Stanford Center on Poverty and Inequality. https://www.stanford.edu/group/recessiontrends/cgi-bin/web/sites/all/themes/barron/pdf/LaborMarkets_fact_sheet.pdf

Ianinska, S., Wright, U., & Rocco, T. S. (2003). *Critical race theory and adult education: Critique of the literature in Adult Education Quarterly*. Paper presented at the meeting of the Second Annual College of Education Research Conference, Florida International University. Retrieved from http://digitalcommons.fiu.edu/sferc/2003/2003/14/

Illich, I. (1973). *Deschooling society*. Harmondsworth, UK: Penguin.

Kena, G., Aud, S., & Johnson, F. (2014). *The condition of education 201*. (Report No. NCES 2014083). Washington, DC: U.S. Department of Education, Institute of Education Sciences, National Center for Education Statistics. Retrieved from http://nces.ed.gov/pubsearch/pubsinfo.asp?pubid=2014083

Kmec, J., & Furstenberg, F. (2002). Racial and gender differences in the transition to adulthood: A longitudinal study of Philadelphia youth. *Advances in Life Course Research, 7*, 435–470. doi:10.1016/S1040-2608(02)80042-9

Knowles, M. S. (1975). *Self-directed learning*. New York: Association Press.

Ladson-Billings, G. (1999). Just what is critical race theory and what is it doing in a nice field like education? In L. Parker, D. Deyhle, & S. Villenas (Eds.), *Race is race isn't: Critical race theories and qualitative studies in education* (pp. 7–30). Boulder, CO: Westview Press.

Merriam, S. (2001). Andragogy and self-directed learning: Pillars of adult learning theory. In S. Merriam (Ed.), *New Directions for Adult and Continuing Education: No. 89. The new update on adult learning theory* (pp. 3–14). San Francisco, CA: Jossey-Bass.

Noguera, P. A., & Boykin, W. A. (2011). *Closing the achievement gap: From research to practice*. Washington, DC: ASCD.

Noguera, P. A., Ayers, W., Ladson-Billings, G., & Stovall, D. (Eds.). (2008). *City kids, city schools*. New York: New Press.

Schwartz, J. (2014). Classrooms of spatial justice: Counter-spaces and young men of color in a GED program. *Adult Education Quarterly, 64*(2), 110–127. doi:10.1177/0741713613513632

Taylor, P., Parker, K., Fry, R., Cohn, D., Wang, W., Velasco, G., et al. (2011). *Is college worth it? College presidents, public access, value, quality and mission of higher education*. Retrieved from http://www.pewsocialtrends.org/2011/05/15/is-college-worth-it/

Tough, A. (1971). *The adult's learning projects: A fresh approach to theory and practice in adult learning*. Toronto: Ontario Institute for Studies in Education.

U.S. Department of Labor. (2015). I. E-16. Washington, DC: Bureau of Labor Statistics, U.S. Department of Labor. Retrieved from http://www.bls.gov/web/empsit/cpsee_e16.htm

Whitsett, H. C. (2012). *High debt, low information: Survey of student loan borrowers*. New York: National Economic Research Associates.

RICHARD OSBORNE is a property management and development professional with expertise in high-end construction, fine dining, and luxury real estate.

JONI SCHWARTZ is an associate professor in the Humanities Department at the City University of New York, LaGuardia Community College.

New Directions for Adult and Continuing Education • DOI: 10.1002/ace

4

The educational role of the Black church is explored along with its role in educating Black males and preparing them for leadership in the community and society.

Black Males in Black Churches

Traci L. Hodges, Michael L. Rowland, E. Paulette Isaac-Savage

Historically in America as Blacks were relegated to low-class citizenship, disrespected, and oppressed, they needed a place to combat societal ills they faced daily. The Black church was that haven (Lincoln & Mamiya, 1990; Rowland & Isaac-Savage, 2014). Mattis et al. (2004) further explain that even today, among other things, the Black church provides political, material, and psychological support. Hence, the historical "church not only served as a place of spiritual worship," it was "a refuge from racism and a location where African Americans could learn values, knowledge, and skills" (Isaac, Guy, & Valentine, 2001, p. 23). To meet the needs of Blacks, the church provided many resources. An important need, which many believed would contribute to the uplift of Blacks, was education (Franklin, 1990). The Black church provided both formal and informal educational opportunities (Isaac, 2009).

In the late 19th and early 20th centuries, many Black churches served as schoolhouses during the week (Lakey, 1996) for children and adults. Black denominations would later expand their formal educational efforts by establishing trade or training schools. For example, today's Tuskegee University was established as Tuskegee Institute. Although some schools would eventually become defunct, many survived, including Wilberforce University, Spelman College, and Payne College, and are still filling a void for many Blacks seeking to further their education. Informally, the Black church offered numerous educational opportunities. In her examination of historical and current programming in the church, Isaac (2002) identified several subject areas taught in the Black church. They included health, personal finance, arts and crafts, and leadership.

Despite the educational opportunities in religious organizations, there are differences between men's and women's participation within them. Women are more active in church than men (Mattis et al., 2004). Women score higher on dimensions of nonorganizational religious involvement, such as reading a bible, and higher on religious organizational involvement (i.e., attending

NEW DIRECTIONS FOR ADULT AND CONTINUING EDUCATION, no. 150, Summer 2016 © 2016 Wiley Periodicals, Inc.
Published online in Wiley Online Library (wileyonlinelibrary.com) • DOI: 10.1002/ace.20185

worship service) (Mattis et al., 2004). Despite the low attendance of Black men in church, Black churches continue to offer educational programs to this underserved group of learners. In this chapter, we explore the Black church's role in educating Black males through a variety of educational programming. We also discuss how the Black church prepares them for leadership.

Education and Employment Needs of Black Men

Black men have been described as an endangered species for decades (Guy, 2014). Guy questioned the lack of steps taken to "preserve, protect, rejuvenate, and animate the talents, abilities, and potential" (p. 17) of Black men. President Obama (2014a) sought to address this issue with the launch of My Brother's Keeper (MBK) Task Force in 2014. The MBK Task Force initiative was created to address high rates of African American male unemployment, incarceration, and victimization due to violence. An MBK Task Force was developed that included the secretaries of government agencies, the Attorney General, and other government officials. The task force was set to address many needs of young men and boys of color. This initiative also addressed specific needs of adult males, which include college and career planning, mentoring, and criminal justice system interactions (Obama, 2014b). It was designed to be a collaborative effort between government, the business community, and not-for-profit and faith-based organizations (Obama, 2014a). President Obama (2014a) has called upon faith communities and public and private sectors to take responsibility for addressing some of the barriers that Black men experience. This makes sense as "some adults have been successful in acquiring marketable skills when they turned to their local church for support and guidance" (Isaac, 2010, p. 125). Furthermore, several churches have ventured into economic development, thus providing job experience for Black adults (Isaac, 2010).

We continue to see disparities between Black and White men. According to the Bureau of Justice Statistics, 37% of prison inmates in 2014 were Black males and 3% of Black men were serving at least a 1-year sentence as compared to .5% of White men (Carson, 2015). "Imprisonment rates for black males were 3.8 to 10.5 times greater at each age group than white males and 1.4 to 3.1 times greater than rates for Hispanic males" (Carson, 2015, p. 15). The incarceration rate of Black men overall is 6 times the rate of White men (Carson, 2015; MBK Task Force, 2014) and is 10 times the rate of White men for ages 18–19 (Carson, 2015). Overrepresentation in the justice system has ripple effects for Black men, which leads to lower career outcomes due to exoffender status, higher mortality rates, less stability in family relationships, and lower marital rates (Council of Economic Advisers [COE], 2015). Interventions are needed to address the educational and employment needs of prisoners reentering society (MBK Task Force, 2014). "A black male born 25 years ago has only a 1 in 2 chance of being employed today as a result of early death, incarceration, low labor force participation and high unemployment" (COE, 2015).

New Directions for Adult and Continuing Education • DOI: 10.1002/ace

Educational Needs. According to the National Center for Education Statistics (2014), 93.5% of Black males 25 to 29 years old completed high school, 20.8% completed a bachelor's degree, and 2.6% completed a master's or higher degree in 2014. However, these rates do not include incarcerated persons as part of the population which overstates the education completion rates (Pettit & Sykes, 2015). "The effect of excluding inmates on estimates of graduation rates has grown over time as the prison and jail population has expanded" (Pettit & Sykes, 2015, p. 601). The MBK Task Force (2014) recommended community-based efforts to develop interventions that address education from early childhood to college. This is significant, because as "Black males negotiate schools, they simultaneously navigate the whirlpools and rough waters of prejudice and bigotry, of . . . hopelessness and despair" (Guy, 2014, p. 18). Regarding secondary and postsecondary education, the task force noted that young men need college advising, assistance with financial aid and college applications, job training, mentoring, and apprenticeship. Barriers were noted regarding persistence in completing post-secondary education and training due to sociocultural factors that lead to feelings of isolation and lack of support. There are systemic barriers related to transferring college credits among institutions and college affordability (MBK Task Force, 2014).

Employment Needs. In the third quarter of 2015, the unemployment rate for Black men 20 years and over was 8.8%, 225% higher than White men (3.9%), and the rate was 33% for Black men 18 to 19 years old, 239% higher than White men (13.8%) (Bureau of Labor Statistics, 2015a). The racial disparity in employment is understated due to the exclusion of incarcerated males or those who experienced an early death and may be as high as a 24 percentage point gap for prime-age men (COE, 2015). Due to rising incarceration rates, "young black men who have dropped out of high school are more likely to be incarcerated than working in the paid labor force" (Pettit & Sykes, 2015, p. 600). Black men make 76.1% of the median weekly earnings of White men for full-time employment (Bureau of Labor Statistics, 2015b). Not surprising, involvement with the criminal justice system, coupled with employment gaps and lack of educational attainment, affects Black males' earnings (COE, 2015). The MBK Task Force (2014) recommended access to internships, job shadowing, and mentoring to enhance social capital and career information. This supported the need for the Black church to enhance its community outreach efforts.

Black Male Initiatives in the Black Church

In 2009, President Obama issued an executive order to create the President's Advisory Council on Faith-Based and Neighborhood Partnerships to brainstorm ways to collaborate with faith-based and neighborhood organizations (Office of Justice Programs, 2015; White House, 2015). "Realizing that no one entity can solve the social ills, the Bush Administration and now the Obama Administration have called on a more deliberate collaboration of faith and community-based organizations" (Rowland & Chappel-Aiken, 2012, p. 25). Centers for Faith-Based and Neighborhood Partnerships are housed in federal agencies to work with community organizations (White House, 2015). The center in the U.S. Department of Justice works with faith-based organizations on prisoner reentry, violence prevention, and promoting responsible fatherhood (Office of Justice Programs, 2015). The U.S. Department of Health and Human Services (USDHHS, 2015) provides support for programs on fatherhood, mentoring, health, and wellness. The U.S. Department of Commerce (2015) provides support for entrepreneurship training and business development opportunities. The U.S. Department of Labor (2015) provides support for job clubs. This network of support can provide resources and opportunities for collaboration with other organizations, as demonstrated later in this chapter.

National Baptist Convention. The National Baptist Convention, USA, Inc. (2015b) met with the White House in 2011 with 86 convention leaders to discuss the faith-based development initiative. As a result, the convention established the "Rising to New Challenges" charge (National Baptist Convention, USA, Inc., 2015b, p. 1). This is an example of how the faith-based initiative can support Black churches in serving the needs of the congregation and local community. The Criminal Justice Commission has an education ministry to reduce interactions with the justice system. Curriculum is available for churches on biblical manhood, preventive parenting, and employment readiness (National Baptist Convention, USA, Inc., 2015a). The convention has created a Health Ambassador Challenge to train 10,000 ambassadors for health promotion programs to support the "H.O.P.E. Initiative of the Congress of Christian Education" (Mayhan, 2012, para. 1).

Fatherhood Programs with Housing and Urban Development. Local housing authority agencies host fatherhood community activities in collaboration with local faith-based and community organizations (U.S. Department of Housing and Urban Development, 2013). The Biloxi (MS) Housing Authority has sponsored four annual fatherhood initiative programs, so that "fathers can gain child development and sustainable life skills while participating in an array of educational, recreational, and social events which will encourage interaction between fathers and their children" (Thompson, 2014, p. 1). These programs were hosted in collaboration with Greater Grace Apostolic Assembly, Cedar Lake Christian Assembly, local businesses, and community organizations, thus illustrating how churches can collaborate with local government agencies and communities to address the needs of Black men.

100 Black Men College to Church Program. Demonstrating how the Black church collaborates with community organizations and educational institutions, the 100 Black Men of Greater Lafayette (LA) collaborated with the South Louisiana Community College (SLCC), Senior Pastors United Alliance, and local churches to host the "College to Church" program (SLCC, 2015) to provide information about admissions, financial aid, and the transfer process. The chancellor stated: "This game-changing program will provide an underserved population of citizens with an entry point to higher education, community and faith based support to help them excel, and the necessary skills to attend and graduate from SLCC" (SLCC, 2015, p. 1). The event was hosted in October 2015 at a local community center.

Sons of Allen. The African Methodist Episcopal Church (AME) has a long tradition of educating its members to face the reality of their situation (Payne, 1866; West, 1994). The Sons of Allen men's ministry program of the AME Church is an example of a holistic ministry that includes adult education for African American men (AME, 2015a). This ministry has five strategic initiatives to serve the needs of male congregants (AME, 2015b). One of the initiatives addresses the needs of men who are reentering society from prison and provides assistance with "job training, job placement, and re-socialization" (AME, 2015b, p. 1). Education and mentoring are also initiatives that support the needs of Black men (AME, 2015b).

Black Church Health Education for Men

The Black church provides health and wellness programs for all members. Some have programs specifically targeting Black men's health. The United Church of Christ (United Church of Christ, 2015), the National Baptist Convention (Hope, 2016), and the AME Church (AMEC, 2015) have developed national health ministries to serve the health and wellness needs of their congregations. This is espoused by Rowland and Isaac-Savage (2014) who stated, the "Black church has served as a vehicle for healthcare and health promotions activities to address the health concerns, needs, and most importantly, the disparities in healthcare that plague the Black community" (p. 19). Prostate cancer educational programs have evolved from printed materials (Holt et al., 2009) to multimedia programs (Emerson, Reece, Levine, Hull, & Husaini, 2009) to active learning programs with peer leaders (Holt et al., 2009; Langford, Griffith, Beasley, & Braxton, 2014).

Prostate Cancer Education. Prostate cancer education programs were enhanced over the years from short-term interventions (Emerson et al., 2009; Holt et al., 2009) to sustainable programming models (Langford et al., 2014). A significant theme for prostate cancer education is the cultural competency of the program facilitators who reflected the men they were attempting to reach. Community health advisors and peers have been used to enhance the facilitation of the programs (Holt et al., 2009). The role of the church evolved from a recruitment source (Langford et al., 2014) to a delivery site (Emerson et al., 2009; Holt et al., 2009) to a site for transformation through the inclusion of spiritual content (Holt et al., 2009).

Southeastern Michigan. The University of Michigan Comprehensive Cancer Center hosted the Men's Fellowship Breakfast (MFB) program in Ypsilanti and Ann Arbor to provide health education to the public community regarding cancer risk reduction. The MFB is a great example of a sustainable programming model and of the use of the African American church or recruitment and outreach. African American men's ministry programs were used for recruitment and some programs hosted events at the MFB location prior to the breakfast to enhance participation. The cancer center hosted 21 events from 2008–2014 with over 425 participants (Langford et al., 2014). Topics included cancer prevention, health promotion, financial literacy, mental health, and estate planning (Langford et al., 2014). This research highlights the need for additional programming within the Black church to address needs beyond prostate cancer in male-only programs.

Nashville, TN. Researchers at Tennessee State University and Meharry Medical College developed a prostate cancer educational intervention program with 45 African American churches in Nashville, TN. The churches were recruited from a sampling frame of 206 African American churches in the area. The intervention was a 1-hour group session that included a video that showcased African American physicians and prostate cancer survivors. An African American physician from Meharry Medical College facilitated a question and answer and informational session. The hosting church organized the logistics and recruitment for the programs. There were 422 African American male participants and 345 of them participated in the 3-month and 6-month follow-up interviews (Emerson et al., 2009). "The study carried out in community settings (i.e., places of worship) and by project staff of the same race and background most likely contributed to the comfort level of the participants and to increased positive responses" (Emerson et al., 2009, p. 344).

Birmingham, AL. The University of Alabama Birmingham Comprehensive Cancer Center conducted research with two Baptist churches to assess the effectiveness of an intervention with spiritual content as compared to a non-spiritual intervention for prostate cancer prevention (Holt et al., 2009). Participants ($n = 49$) were recruited using church resources, such as bulletins, flyers, announcements, and information on monitors. The church pastors designated a community health advisor (CHA) to receive training and facilitate the educational programs. The CHAs were trained, formally assessed for knowledge and presentation skills and certified by the research team. The programs were conducted at convenient times for participants using a 1-hour Sunday school format with printed materials. The materials contained spiritual content for the groups receiving the spiritual intervention (Holt et al., 2009). "Men who attended the spiritually based session reported reading significantly more of the printed materials than those who attended the non-spiritual session" (Holt et al., 2009, p. 257). This research highlights the benefits of using the church beyond recruitment and program hosting. The use of spiritual content can enhance the relevance of adult education content.

Funding for Faith-Based Programs for Black Men

There is a lack of partnerships between philanthropic organizations and faith organizations despite being considered an "untapped resource that can be more deeply engaged in the field" by stakeholders for black male achievement

(Shah & Sato, 2014, p. 33). In 2012, $64.6 million was distributed for grants for Black men and boys initiatives and only 1% was distributed to science organizations and religious institutions (BMAfunders, 2015). Black churches can seek opportunities to collaborate with public affairs and human service organizations and educational institutions that receive 92% of grant funding. Municipal governments also receive grant funding and can be potential partners for collaborative programming. In 2012, $20 million and 30% of grant funds were distributed for education and 89% of funds were used for program support (BMAfunders, 2015). Adult educators can serve as resources to Black churches to help with program planning and collaboration with community organizations and educational institutions to engage with philanthropic organizations.

Black Church and Leadership

The Black church has been a breeding ground for many Black male leaders. In fact, Black leaders gained their training in the Black church (Lincoln & Mamiya, 1990). By serving in such roles as deacons, lay leaders, and trustees, many Blacks were able to develop leadership skills (Este, 2004; Franklin, 2007). Well-known individuals like Martin L. King, Jr., Jesse Jackson, Jr. and Al Sharpton began their social activism training in the church. Yet, although the Black church and many of its male leaders have been at the forefront of many sociopolitical movements, they have been less progressive in their promotion of female clergy as leaders (Taylor & Chatters, 2010). Much of this may be attributed to church doctrine and theological differences in the role of men and women in the church. However, it has been estimated that the majority of Black church congregants are female (Corbie-Smith et al., 2010; Taylor & Chatters, 2010). Some male church leaders believe in the more biblical roles of men and women in the church. Traditionally, leadership positions, particularly of Black pastors in the Black church, were borne out of a "call" from God to lead a church (Hoover, 2012) and less from a vocational aspiration.

Today, Black church leadership requires more from the pastor than just being a religious leader; the pastoral leader must also be a community leader and often an activist. The leadership of the Black church must be politically savvy in order to make good decisions for the community and to deal with crises within the Black community. This certainly exemplified Rev. Clementa Pinckey, one of the nine killed in Emmanuel AME in Charleston, South Carolina. Black church leaders must understand financial and accounting operations of the church, manage a church staff, and understand how to cultivate and promote church membership. Black church leadership must be prepared to handle the physical and emotional needs of the church membership and community. It is therefore incumbent on Black church leaders to prepare themselves not just spiritually but also attend seminary institutions and learn how to become an effective spiritual leader of the Black church.

Summary

The Black church will continue to play a significant role in the lives of African Americans. This has been manifested in Ferguson, MO, and Charleston, SC, with the killing of a young Black male and nine Black parishioners, respectively. Within the past 12 months, Black church leaders have demonstrated how the church responds to the needs of the Black community. They have been in the midst of protests and have held community meetings and forums. With the perpetual attack on African American men, "adult educators are needed to facilitate the transition through the stages of critical consciousness. We must enhance the critical reflection process so individuals," such as Black men, "can be empowered to solve local problems" (Hodges, 2015, p. 2).

Adult educators can play a significant role in the establishment of church-based programs that help not only Black men but the Black community in general. Adult educators who understand and who are knowledgeable in teaching methodologies and learning can design effective programs and assess outcomes. In establishing programs for Black males in the community, particularly in the Black church, consideration should be given to identifying key community leaders, who know the pulse of the community and can help recruit Black men; building relationships not only with the pastor but with others in the community that the church serves; taking the time to assess the community's needs; providing culturally relevant learning, which includes culturally relevant curriculum; and establishing, with stakeholders, clear program outcomes and assessment measures (Rowland & Chappel-Aiken, 2012). Although some may question the importance of the Black church today, it does make a difference in the lives of Black males. As discussed in this chapter, there are examples of programs and initiatives educating and preparing Black men. These programs provide a plethora of research and educational opportunities for adult educators.

References

African Methodist Episcopal Church. (2015a, October 13). *Sons of Allen: Men's fellowship of the African Methodist Episcopal Church*. Retrieved from http://www.amesonsofallen.org/3/miscellaneous1.htm

African Methodist Episcopal Church. (2015b, October 13). *The sons of Allen: Strategic initiatives*. Retrieved from http://www.amesonofallen.org/3/miscellaneous5.htm

AMEC. (2015). *About the AME health commission*. Retrieved from http://www.ourhealt hministry.com/Ministries-and-Groups/Denominations/AME/AMEC-Home/About-AMEC

BMAfunders. (2015). *Quantifying hope: Philanthropic support for Black men and boys*. New York: Author.

Bureau of Labor Statistics. (2015a). *Usual weekly earnings of wage and salary workers second quarter 2015* [Press release]. Retrieved from http://www.bls.gov/news.release/archives/wkyeng_07212015.pdf

Bureau of Labor Statistics. (2015b). *Household data not seasonally adjusted quarterly averages: Unemployment rates by age, sex, race, and Hispanic or Latino ethnicity (E-16)*. Retrieved from http://www.bls.gov/web/empsit/cpsee_e16.htm

Carson, E. A. (2015). *Prisoners in 2014 (Bulletin NCJ 248955)*. Washington, DC: U.S. Department of Justice, Bureau of Justice Statistics.

Corbie-Smith, G., Goldmon, M., Isler, M. R., Washington, C., Ammerman, A., Green, M., et al. (2010). Partnerships in health disparities research and the roles of pastors of black churches: Potential conflict, synergy, and expectations. *Journal of the National Medical Association, 102*(9), 823–831.

Council of Economic Advisers. (2015). *Economic costs of youth disadvantage and high-return opportunities for change*. Washington, DC: Executive Office of the President.

Emerson, J. S., Reece, M. C., Levine, R. S., Hull, P.C., & Husaini, B. A. (2009). Predictors of new screening for African American men participating in a prostate cancer educational program. *Journal of Cancer Education, 24*(4), 341–345. doi: 10.1080/08858190902854749

Este, D. C. (2004). The Black church as a social welfare institution: Union United Church and the development of Montreal's Black community, 1907–1940. *Journal of Black Studies, 35*(1), 3–22.

Franklin, R. M. (2007). *Crisis in the village: Restoring hope in African American communities*. Minneapolis, MN: Fortress Press.

Franklin, V. P. (1990). Education for life: Adult education programs for African Americans in northern cities, 1900–1942. In H. G. Neufeldt & L. McGee (Eds.), *Education of the African American adult: An historical overview* (pp. 113–134). New York: Greenwood Press.

Guy, T. C. (2014). The (end)angered Black male swimming against the current. In D. Rosser-Mims, J. Schwartz, B. Drayton, & T. C. Guy (Eds.), *New Directions for Adult and Continuing Education: No. 144. Swimming upstream: Black makes in adult education* (pp. 15–26). San Francisco, CA: Jossey-Bass.

Holt, C., Wynn, T., Litaker, M., Southward, P., Jeames, S., & Schulz, E. (2009). A comparison of a spiritually based and non-spiritually based educational intervention for informed decision making for prostate cancer screening among church-attending African American men. *Urologic Nursing, 29*(4), 249–258.

Hodges, T. L. (2015). Public spaces of protest framed with adult learning and political efficacy: Reflections of a freedom summer in Madrid and Ferguson. *Adult Learning*. Retrieved from http://alx.sagepub.com/content/early/2015/07/03/1045159515595042.full.pdf?ijkey=UBkcsBGxXKBtp7d&keytype=finitehin

Hoover, J. A. (2012). Thy daughters shall prophesy: The Assemblies of God, inerrancy, and the question of clergywomen. *Journal of Pentecostal Theology, 21*(2), 221–239.

HOPE. (2016). *National Baptist Convention, USA Inc. HOPE HHS partnership: About*. Retrieved from http://www.hopenbc.com/about.

Isaac, E. P. (2009). Lyceum Guild: A ministry on a mission. *Journal of Traditions and Beliefs, 1*(1), 21–32.

Isaac, E. P. (2010). The role of the Black church in developing congregants for the workplace. In M. V. Alfred (Ed.), *Learning for economic self-sufficiency: Constructing pedagogies of hope among low-income, low literate adults* (pp. 121–132). Charlotte, NC: Information Age Publishing.

Isaac, E. P., Guy, T., & Valentine, T. (2001). Understanding African American adult learners' motivations to learn in church-based adult education. *Adult Education Quarterly, 52*(1), 23–38.

Isaac, P. (2002). The adult education phase of the African American church revisited. *Christian Education Journal, 6*(1), 7–23.

Lakey, O. H. (1996). *The history of the CME church* (Rev.). Memphis, TN: CME Publishing House.

Langford, A., Griffith, D., Beasley, D., & Braxton, E. (2014). A cancer center's approach to engaging African American men about cancer: The men's fellowship breakfast, southeastern Michigan, 2008–2014. *Preventing Chronic Disease, 11*, 140187. Retrieved from http://www.cdc.gov/pcd/issues/2014/14_0187.htm

Lincoln, C. E., & Mamiya, L. H. (1990). *The Black church in the African American experience.* Durham, NC: Duke University Press.

Mattis, J., Beckham, W., Saunders, B., Williams, J., McAllister, D., Myers, V., et al. (2004). Who will volunteer? Religiosity, everyday racism, and social participation among African American men. *Journal of Adult Development, 11*(4), 261–272.

Mayhan, D. (2012). *The First Lady's 10,000 health ambassador challenge.* Retrieved from http://www.nationalbaptist.com/departments/living-with-hope-blog/the-first-ladys-10,000-health-ambassador-challenge.html

My Brother's Keeper Task Force. (2014). *Report to the President.* Washington, DC: Author.

National Baptist Convention, USA, Inc. (2015a, October 13). *Education ministry of the criminal justice commission.* Retrieved from http://www.nationalbaptist.com/departments/criminal-justice-commission/education-ministry.html

National Baptist Convention, USA, Inc. (2015b, October 13). *History of the faith based development initiative.* Retrieved from http://www.nationalbaptist.com/departments/faith-based-development-initiative/about-the-faith-based-initiative.html

National Center for Education Statistics. (2014). *Percentage of persons 25 to 29 years old with selected levels of educational attainment, by race/ethnicity and sex: Selected years 1920 through 2014.* Retrieved from https://nces.ed.gov/programs/digest/d13/tables/dt13_104.20.asp

Obama, B. H. (2014a, February 27). *Presidential memorandum-Creating and expanding ladders of opportunity for boys and young men of color* [Press release]. Retrieved from https://www.whitehouse.gov/the-press-office/2014/02/27/presidential-memorandum-creating-and-expanding-ladders-opportunity-boys-

Obama, B. H. (2014b, February 27). *Remarks by the President on "My Brother's Keeper" Initiative* [Press release]. Retrieved from https://www.whitehouse.gov/the-press-office/2014/02/27/remarks-president-my-brothers-keeper-initiative

Office of Justice Programs. (2015, October 13). *White House Office of FBNP.* Retrieved from http://ojp.gov/fbnp/administration.htm

Payne, D. A. (1866). *The semi-centenary and the retrospection of the African Methodist Episcopal church.* Baltimore, MD: Sherwood & Co.

Pettit, B., & Sykes, B. L. (2015). Civil rights legislation and legalized exclusion: Mass incarceration and the masking of inequality. *Sociological Forum, 30*(S1), 589–611.

Rowland, M., & Chappel-Aiken, L. (2012). Faith-based partnerships promoting health. In E. P. Isaac (Ed.), *New Directions for Adult and Continuing Education: No. 133. Expanding the boundaries of adult religious education: Strategies techniques, and partnerships for the new millennium* (pp. 23–33). San Francisco, CA: Jossey-Bass.

Rowland, M., & Isaac-Savage, P. (2014). The Black church: Promoting health, fighting disparities. In J. C. Collins, L. O. Bryant, & T. S. Rocco (Eds.), *New Directions for Adult and Continuing Education: No. 142. Health and wellness concerns for racial, ethnic, and sexual minorities* (pp. 15–24). San Francisco, CA: Jossey-Bass.

Shah, S., & Sato, G. (2014). *Building a beloved community: Strengthening the field of Black male achievement.* New York: Foundation Center.

South Louisiana Community College. (2015, October 2). *New venue for "College to Church" event Oct. 10.* Retrieved from http://solacc.edu/content/new-venue-college-church-event-oct-10

Taylor, R., & Chatters, L. (2010). Importance of religion & spirituality in the lives of African Americans, Caribbean Blacks, and Non-Hispanic Whites. *Journal of Negro Education, 79*(3), 280–294.

Thompson, K. (2014). *Fatherhood initiative celebration.* Retrieved from http://www.biloxi.ms.us/agendas/citycouncil/2014/052014/052014bexc.pdf

United Church of Christ. (2015). *United Church of Christ: Health.* Retrieved from http://www.ucc.org/health.

U.S. Department of Commerce. (2015, October 14). *Center for Faith-Based and Neighborhood Partnerships*. Retrieved from http://www.commerce.gov/office-secretary/center-faith-based-and-neighborhood-partnerships

U.S. Department of Health and Human Services. (2015, October 14). *The Center for Faith-Based and Neighborhood Partnerships*. Retrieved from http://hhs.gov/partnerships/

U.S. Department of Housing and Urban Development. (2013). *Father's Day 2013: Re-connecting families and dads*. Retrieved from http://portal.hud.gov/hudportal/documents/huddoc?id=rfd2013slideshow.pdf

U.S. Department of Labor. (2015, October 14). *Center for Faith-Based and Neighborhood Partnerships (CFBNP)*. Retrieved from http://www.dol.gov/cfbnp/

West, A. M. G. (1994). *African Methodist Episcopal pastoral perceptions concerning the role of the church in adult education*. Dissertation Abstracts International, 55-09A:2687. (UMI No. AAI9503114)

White House. (2015). *About the Office of Faith-Based and Neighborhood Partnerships*. Retrieved from https://whitehouse.gov/administration/eop/ofbnp/about

TRACI L. HODGES is a former accounting instructor and currently a career consultant and PhD candidate in the educational leadership and policy studies program at the University of Missouri-St. Louis.

MICHAEL L. ROWLAND is an associate professor in the Department of Internal Medicine and the associate dean for faculty affairs at the University of Kentucky College of Medicine.

E. PAULETTE ISAAC-SAVAGE is a professor of adult education and associate provost for planning and assessment at the University of Missouri-St. Louis.

New Directions for Adult and Continuing Education • DOI: 10.1002/ace

5

In this chapter the authors examine the role of spirituality in the lives of Black gay men.

Adult Education and Spirituality: A "Liberatory Spaces" for Black Gay Men

Lawrence Bryant, Lorenzo Bowman, E. Paulette Isaac-Savage

Mainstream adult education has historically dedicated little effort to addressing spiritual issues related to Black gay men. Without a voice in the research literature, Black gay men are silent and invisible when it comes to expressing their sexuality and their spirituality. This chapter examines the spiritually based life experiences of Black gay men at the intersection of race, class, and sexual identity. We highlight the critical role adult educators can play in assisting learners in meaning-making under conditions that are in conflict with dominant ideologies (Hill, 2002). We conclude with an exploration of findings from three autoethnographies. Findings from the analysis of the three autoethnographies indicate that Black gay men conceal feelings, are indoctrinated in the Black church at an early age, and consider spirituality an integral part of their daily lives. However, in their quest for individuality and self-expression, Black gay men have found "Liberatory Spaces" in the form of reconciliation and reinterpretation of former religious teachings. Sheared and Sissel (2001) operationalized "Making Spaces" as an action undertaken by both learner and adult educator, which involves acknowledging the invisibility, inequities, and oppressive forces that marginalized communities face on a daily basis. Providing opportunities and space in the academy and community for their voices to be heard is an expectation of "Making Spaces." To this end, we seek to make space for Black gay men to share their experiences, find their voices, and challenge the hegemonic dominant ideologies regarding sexuality, spirituality, and race.

When Black gay men discuss spirituality in learning circles, we see a contentious relationship between them and the ideologies about homosexuality that prevail in Black communities. Although the American Psychological Association (APA) and most mental health experts agree that homosexuality is a psychological predisposition not born of a psychological defect or mental illness, many in the Black community are not convinced and often

NEW DIRECTIONS FOR ADULT AND CONTINUING EDUCATION, no. 150, Summer 2016 © 2016 Wiley Periodicals, Inc.
Published online in Wiley Online Library (wileyonlinelibrary.com) • DOI: 10.1002/ace.20186

discriminate against the Black gay community (Bryant, 2008; Griffin, 2006; Leland & Miller, 1998).

Discrimination against Black Gay Men

Oppression can take many forms, including legal, social, economic, educational, religious, and political systems in America (Delgado, 1989). Values such as individuality, freedom of expression, economic security and community acceptance are elusive and, at best, fleeting for many Black gay men (Boyd, 1996; Bush, 1999; Johnson & Henderson, 2005; Whitehead, 1997). Strictures against homosexual relationships in the Black community have given rise to discrimination in the form of homophobia, a term used in this chapter to identify an irrational fear of homosexuals (Griffin, 2006). Moreover, because homophobia is prevalent in the Black community, most Black gay men have a much more tangled maze to navigate regarding their sexuality and sexual orientation (Bryant, 2008).

The Black Church, Homophobia, and Black Gay Men

In many instances, the practice of homosexuality in the Black community is strictly forbidden (Bryant, 2008; Hill, 1995). Homophobia may come from the very place where many Blacks seek refuge—the Black church. Although homosexual relationships have been discouraged throughout American history, they have been especially derided by the Black church (Boykin, 2005; Griffin, 2006). Although the Black church has served as a crucial institution in the education and support of Blacks (Isaac, Rowland, & Blackwell, 2007), it may actually have served as a primary mechanism in the maintenance of Black homophobia and much of the internalized homophobia many Black gay men experience (West, 2001). The Black church's position on homosexuality has mostly been one of condemnation, scorn, and ridicule (Bryant, 2008; Griffin, 2006). Because of these strong oppositional forces, many Black gay men find themselves hiding their true sexuality (King, 2004). However, as the epicenter of Black culture, the Black church could play a central role in providing a safe space for Black gay men to deal with compelling issues, such as social justice, the escalating HIV/AIDS epidemic, and discrimination based on race.

Discrimination and racism do not exist in a vacuum. They come with distinctive historical customs, practices, and belief systems. Many African Americans recognize prejudices based on color but fail to recognize other prejudices, such as sexism, classism, and homophobia. Constantine-Simms (2001) made the following point about homophobia in the Black community:

> It will only change when more Black men realize that Black gay bashing will win no brownie points with White conservatives and will certainly not make them any more sympathetic to Black causes. Former Nation of Islam national spokesperson Khalid Muhammad found that out. In a widely publicized speech

in 1993, he made one of the most devastating and disgusting public assaults
ever on gays. Yet he is still one of the most vilified Black men in America. (p. 5)

What many African Americans fail to realize is that homophobia, racism, classism, and sexism reside within the same dysfunctional belief system. For example, many Black intellectuals collaborate with White conservatives against Black gay men, forgetting that many of these same people are also bigoted, racist, and classist (Boykin, 1996; Constantine-Simms, 2001). Black gay men must challenge these hegemonic forces and find liberatory spaces and ways to cope, and even to thrive, under these circumstances. Some Black gay men have found these spaces through searching for and cultivating their spirituality.

Black Gay Men and Spirituality

There have been many studies conducted in an effort to understand the role of spirituality in the lives of adults (Tisdell, 2000; 2001). Some adult educators have looked at religiosity, because it is easy to observe and quantify. Religion has often been used interchangeably with spirituality. However, the terms have two distinct meanings. Religion has been defined as a "formalized set of ideological commitments associated with a group" (Fincham, Ajayi, & Beach, 2011, p. 260). In other words, individuals who are religious follow certain practices and rituals and maintain certain beliefs associated with an organized group (i.e., denomination). Captured another way, religiosity is the outward sign of the spiritual, including activities such as attendance at churches, synagogues, and mosques. In general, researchers suggest, there is an increase in religiosity over the life span, with a short period of health-related decline at the end of life (Benjamins, Musick, Gold, & George, 2003; Idler, 2006; Idler et al., 2003).

Spirituality can be more difficult to articulate because it can be conceptualized in different ways (Patton & McClure, 2009). We propose some definitions here. "Spirituality is a yearning to connect with community, a higher power, or a transcendent energy, and to liberate this energy within one's self" (Fenwick & Lange, 1998, p. 64). Fenwick and Lange (1998) further explained that spirituality is based on a personal relationship with a higher power, but contains some elements of a person's religious upbringing as well. It can refer to "the personal, subjective side of one's religious experience" (Fincham, Ajayi, & Beach, 2011, p. 260). As such, spirituality may include belief in a transformational life (Mattis et al., 2001). Jagers and Smith (1996) associated spirituality with the African Diaspora and stated that African American spirituality is a worldview composed of cultural expressions central to the Diaspora (Riggins, McNeal, & Herndon, 2008). Pargament (1999), using a psychological lens, took the definitions of spirituality and religion a step further and described them as two domains, proximal and distal, respectively. The proximal domain "measures the functions of religion/spirituality" for individuals

(Shannon, Oakes, Scheers, Richardson, & Stills, 2012, pp. 2–3), whereas the distal domain primarily focuses on behavioral activities, such as prayer and church attendance. Although religion and spirituality are sometimes used interchangeably, we contend that there is a clear demarcation between the two terms.

There are some differences in religiosity based on gender, race, and ethnicity. Women seem to attend church at a higher rate than men do for all ages, all religions, and all countries (Miller & Stark, 2002). Yet older African American women rate spirituality as more important than do older Black men (Taylor, Chatters, & Joe, 2011). In addition, Bryant (2007) and Hammermeister et al. (2005) found women to be more spiritual than men. African Americans and Mexican Americans have higher levels of religious participation than all other groups in the United States (Taylor, Chatters, & Levin, 2004). Wink and Dillon (2002) found that men and women between their mid 50s and mid 70s have an increase in spirituality and a tendency to turn inward as they seek to make spiritual meaning of their lives. They concluded that this is because as we age, we become ever more conscious of the reality that life is finite. Indeed, the adult development research literature reveals that as we age, the notion of time shifts from being infinite to finite (Bjorklund & Bee, 2008). Thus, it would appear that as adults age, they first have to define spirituality for themselves and then seek ways to live it out in their lives. Black gay men are no different; they also seek spiritual meaning-making in an effort to find solace and liberatory spaces in their lives. However, the spiritual search is particularly problematic for Black gay men navigating midlife.

Spirituality in the Lives of Black Gay Men Navigating Midlife

Although many Black gay men are active in Black churches, they are still marginalized as active church members (Bryant, 2008; Griffin, 2006). Many are restricted from holding leadership positions within the church hierarchy. Moreover, they remain a group that receives very little attention or acknowledgment for their contribution to the development and growth of the Black church (Bryant, 2008). Black gay men's stories as exemplified through autoethnographies may help adult educators find ways to assist this vulnerable population to find liberatory spaces. The authors sought to excavate the complexities, intricacies, and difficulties of Black gay men as they navigate toward midlife.

Black gay men live at the nexus of intersecting systems of oppression—race, class, gender identity, and sexual orientation. How do Black gay men learn to sustain their spirituality yet circumnavigate a racist and heterosexist society and faith community? Autoethnographies, as examined through the lens of Black gay men approaching midlife, can help explain this arduous and sometimes confounded process. The purpose of this chapter is to examine the lived experiences of three Black gay men in the development of their spirituality as they grow older.

New Directions for Adult and Continuing Education • DOI: 10.1002/ace

Emergence into Midlife. According to Mezirow (2000), the goal of adult education should be to help learners critically reflect on and effectively act on their beliefs, interpretations, values, feelings, and ways of thinking. Adult education, through social justice principles, has within its academic structure a potential for the adult learner to become liberated from self-limiting belief patterns that inhibit growth and development. In other words, adult education provides a potential for the learner to become transformed and liberated. What does this mean to the adult learner? Mezirow (2000) described an emancipated person as "free from unwarranted control of undesirable beliefs, unsupportable attitudes, and paucity of abilities, which can prevent one from taking charge of one's life." He further stated, "Fostering these liberating conditions [for] making more autonomous and informed choices and developing a sense of self-empowerment is the cardinal goal of adult education" (p. 26).

Through an autoethnographic lens, the authors sought to answer the question: How do Black gay men reconcile their spirituality and religious beliefs with their sexual orientation? This research used concepts from a transformative learning perspective. Transformative learning theory helps us better understand how this marginalized community makes meaning and uses critical reflection in addressing heterosexism and oppression (Taylor, 2008).

Autoethnography involves an insider's perspective on a cultural event or group. The insider has intimate knowledge of the event or group (Ellis & Bochner, 2003). Autoethnography connects the personal to the cultural, using various methodological strategies (Ellis & Bochner, 2003). This type of research leads to a deeper understanding of the researcher's personal experience by using techniques such as introspection and by focusing on feelings, thoughts, and culture (Esterberg, 2002).

Findings

Relevant themes, patterns, and observations related to the three ethnographies emerged as the data were rigorously examined and compared. Content analysis of the autoethnographies revealed six common themes related to spirituality in the lives of the participants: Active Concealment, Early Black Church Indoctrination, Reinterpretation and Reconciliation, Embraced Spirituality, and Evolved Altruism. After a brief description of the participants, each theme is discussed.

The three participants have similar backgrounds. They range in age from mid 40s to late 50s. They live in a large southeastern metropolitan area in the United States. Two of the participants possess terminal degrees, and one has a master's degree. Each works in higher education. One participant is an administrator, and the other two are members of the academy. Currently, each participant engages in formal religious/spiritual practices. Moreover, they have maintained regular affiliation with their respective churches throughout their lives. Larry attends a Black nondenominational church and has been a member for many years. Most of the members at his church are gay affirming. Lorenzo has been a member of his Black Catholic church for 30 years; he describes the church as Africentric and welcoming. Frank (pseudonym) attends church regularly but has not maintained a commitment to one particular church.

Active Concealment. An internal spiritual struggle began at an early age for each participant when each boy became aware of a same-sex attraction. Active concealment of feelings had a dual purpose—one to hide true feelings for same-sex attractions, and the other to conceal lack of interest in young male-oriented activities. This conflict manifested itself in many ways, but, for all three participants, hiding their true feelings motivated them to engage in "masculine" activities, such as playing sports and dating girls. Their stories revealed that although they played sports, each did so in order to meet societal expectations.

Frank, Larry, and Lorenzo asserted that they were cognizant of their same-sex attraction at an early age. Frank did not recall the exact age that he realized he had a same-sex attraction, but he did recall knowing that he was "different" at about age 5. He further noted that he did not share the same interests as his brothers and male cousins his age. As a child, Frank played baseball and would intentionally strike out each time he came to bat—he did not like playing. After one game, his father yelled at him "for not doing his best." After that experience, Frank never played the game again. For Larry and Lorenzo, playing sports provided an opportunity for male intimacy that each found enjoyable, even though neither enjoyed playing the sport for itself.

Early Black Church Indoctrination. All three men were required to attend church regularly at a very early age without exception. The families' expectation speaks to the centrality of the Black Church in their lives. Each boy sought to make spiritual meaning of his sexual orientation early on. Frank grew up in a very religious home and was very involved in church. He was an active participant in the youth church and youth choir. He always enjoyed singing in the church choir, so much that he wanted to become the choir director. He recalled putting on his mother's choir robe and standing in front of the mirror pretending that he was the choir director and "shouting" like the ladies in the church. Larry also attended church at an early age and was involved in the choir and related church activities, such as Bible Training Union (BTU). Most important, the boys' involvement in church from youth meant that each participant was taught early on that homosexuality was sinful, an abomination, and a violation of the "natural" laws of God.

Reinterpretation and Reconciliation. After moving into adulthood, the participants reconciled their churches' teachings with their personal realities as Black gay men, which required a critical, historical reinterpretation of the Bible as opposed to the literal approach. Interestingly, no one considered rejecting church teachings until adulthood. During his freshman year in college, Lorenzo rejected the teachings of his mother's church regarding homosexuality and its view of sacred scripture. He sought out other faith communities that nurtured his spirituality and fostered a healthy self-identity. Frank similarly rejected the teachings of the church regarding his sexual orientation.

New Directions for Adult and Continuing Education • DOI: 10.1002/ace

He researched the interpretation of sacred Christian writings and the Bible for himself and came to understand the Bible from a different, affirming perspective. He concluded that most of what he had been taught about the Bible was interpreted from a literal perspective, as opposed to a cultural–historical perspective. Like the others, Larry rejected the teachings of the church and sought a denomination that was inclusive and understood God as he had come to understand Him based on his life experiences. He came to understand God as a loving and caring entity that embraced his sexual orientation as part of his humanness. Larry further noted the intrinsic nature of his sexuality as something that he could not, and did not want, to change.

Embraced Spirituality. As with many adults, spirituality was central to the lives of Larry, Lorenzo, and Frank. Spirituality, not religion, is integral in their lives today, in spite of the homophobic teachings they experienced from church and family. For example, as far back as he could remember, Frank "always had a close relationship with the most-high God." Similarly, Larry recalled the role spirituality played in helping him overcome many challenges in his life, including drug addiction and obtaining a PhD. He stated, "As I began to grow spiritually, I began to feel more and more that God saved my life for a reason." Lorenzo came to believe that "God in His creative plan has indeed created some individuals to be gay." Each considered their sexual orientation not to be a choice; rather, it was a part of their God-given identity. A loving and caring God did not and could not give them a "sinful" identity. Thus, each man embraced spirituality as a necessary component intertwined with his self-identity.

Evolved Altruism. Based on their embraced spirituality, all three participants felt a need to give back to others, particularly members of the Black community. Larry felt as if his life had come full circle; that now he could use all of his experiences to give back to a world that he once took so much from. He stated, "I want to make a difference in the lives of Black gay men and the Black community overall." Frank wants to become a mentor and to advise "young Black brothers and sisters to reach their full potential." Lorenzo has a need to help other Black gay men and lesbians by "speaking up." He indicated that he now understands that "silence can be dangerous where oppression is present." He further noted that speaking up challenges the status quo and heteronormative assumptions. Each felt compelled to reach out and help others, especially in reconciling their belief in God with their sexual identity.

Implications for Adult Education

The findings in these autoethnographies have significant implication for those in adult education who support and encourage learning from a social justice and inclusionary perspective. Grace (2001) provides strategies that adult educators can use to provide liberatory space. For example, he posits that queer cultural studies might provide space whereby lesbian, gay, bisexual, and transgenders can find freedom from oppression, and, in the process, transform their lives. He further notes that Queer persons challenge a heterosexist positionality that does not respect their humanity, limits their freedoms, and maintains the status quo through silence, inequality, and invisibility. Similarly, through reconciliation and reinterpretation, Black gay men have challenged this status quo and have found their own interpretation and understanding of liberation and spirituality that affirmed their sexual orientation and identity.

The lived realities of Black gay men (and Black lesbians) have historically been excluded from the research literature in adult education (Grace, 2001). Hill (2007) affirms this oversight as problematic, an ongoing challenge in keeping with our profession's purpose. Although there has been some positive action in the field in recent years through the inclusion of scholarship that has served to reveal the lived realities of lesbian and gay men and women in our society, this scholarship has not typically addressed the unique realities of Black gay men.

Results of our study support the existing literature, which posits that Black gay men consider religion and/or spirituality an important part of their lives and identity (Bryant, 2008; Woodyard, Peterson, & Stokes, 2000); however, many still feel unaccepted and isolated from their cultural mainstream. Traditional theological interpretation supports the belief that all nonheterosexual behaviors are immoral and should be changed to heterosexual. For many Black gay men, this belief has resulted in bondage, legalism, ostracism, depression, alienation, psychiatric institutional admission, violence, despondency, and suicide (Helminiak, 1995). As participants in this study navigated midlife, they searched and found their own interpretation and understanding of spirituality and scriptural interpretation that affirmed their sexual orientation and identity.

Although the spiritual development literature has grown significantly over the past few years, very little, if any, has addressed spiritual development in lesbian, gay bisexual, transgender (LGBT) individuals. None of it has addressed spiritual development in Black gay men. The findings presented in this chapter will provide adult educators with some insight into the spiritual development of Black gay men and with useful knowledge of how this population creates spiritual meaning for themselves in a world that uses religion, heterosexism, and discrimination as tools of oppression.

References

Benjamins, M. R., Musick, M. A., Gold, D. T., & George, L. K. (2003). Age-related declines in activity level: The relationship between chronic illness and religious activities. *Journals of Gerontology, 58*, 377–385.

Bjorklund, B. R., & Bee, H. L. (2008). *The journey of adulthood* (6th ed.). New Upper Saddle River, NJ: Pearson Education.

Boyd, T. (1996). A small introduction to the "G" funk era: Gangsta rap and Black masculinity in contemporary Los Angeles. *Rethinking Los Angeles, 8*, 127–146.

Boykin, K. (1996). *One more river to cross: Black and gay in America.* New York: Random House.

Boykin, K. (2005). *Beyond the down-low: Sex, lies and denial.* New York: Carroll & Graf.

Bryant, A. N. (2007). Gender differences in spiritual development during the college years. *Sex Roles, 56*(11–12), 835–846. doi:10.1007/s11199-007-9240-2

Bryant, L. (2008). *How Black men who have sex with men learn to cope with homophobia and racism.* Unpublished doctoral dissertation, University of Georgia, Athens.

Bush, L. V. (1999). Am I a man? A literature review engaging the sociohistorical dynamics of Black manhood in the United States. *Western Journal of Black Studies, 23*(1), 49–57.

Constantine-Simms, D. (2001). Is homosexuality the greatest taboo? In D. Constantine-Simms (Ed.), *The greatest taboo: Homosexuality in the Black community* (pp. 76–87). Los Angeles, CA: Alyson Books.

Delgado, R. (1989). Storytelling for oppositionists and others: A plea for narrative. *Michigan Law Review, 87,* 2411–2441.

Ellis, C., & Bochner, A. P. (2003). Autobiography, personal narrative, reflexivity: Researcher as subject. In N. K. Denzin & Y. S. Lincoln (Eds.), *Collecting and interpreting qualitative materials* (2nd ed., pp. 199–258). Thousand Oaks, CA: Sage.

Esterberg, K. G. (2002). *Qualitative methods in social research.* New York: McGraw-Hill.

Fenwick, T., & Lange, E. (1998). Spirituality in the workplace: The new frontier of HRD. *Canadian Journal for the Study of Adult Education, 12*(1), 63–87.

Fincham, F. D., Ajayi, C., & Beach, S. R. H. (2011). Spirituality and marital satisfaction in African American couples. *Psychology of Religion and Spirituality, 3*(4), 259–268. doi:10.1037/a0023909

Grace, A. P. (2001). Using queer cultural studies to transgress adult educational space. In V. Sheared & V. Sissel (Eds.), *Making space: Merging theory and practice in adult education* (pp. 257–270). Westport, CT: Greenwood Publishing Group.

Griffin, H. L. (2006). *Their own received them not.* Cleveland, OH: Pilgrim Press.

Hammermeister, J., Flint, M., El-Alayli, A., Ridnour, H., & Peterson, M. (2005). Gender differences in spiritual well-being: Are females more spiritually-well than males? *American Journal of Health Studies, 20*(2), 80–84.

Helminiak, A. D. (1995). *What the Bible really says about homosexuality.* San Francisco, CA: Alamo Square Press.

Hill, R. J. (1995). Gay discourse in adult education: A critical review. *Adult Education Quarterly, 45*(2), 142–158.

Hill, R. J. (2002). Pulling up grassroots: A study of the right-wing "popular" adult environmental education movement in the USA. *Studies in Continuing Education, 24*(2), 181–203.

Hill, R. J. (2007). Breaking open our times (and other liberatory acts). In K. B. Armstrong & L. W. Nabb (Eds.), *American adult educators: Quintessential autobiographies by educators of the 21st century* (pp. 153–158). Chicago, IL: Discovery Association Publishing House.

Idler, E. L. (2006). Religion and aging. In R. H. Binstock & L. K. George (Eds.), *Handbook of aging and the social sciences* (pp. 277–300). San Diego, CA: Academic Press.

Idler, E. L., Musick, M. A., Ellison, C. G., George, L. K., Krause, N., Ory, M. G., et al. (2003). Measuring multiple dimensions of religion and spirituality for health research. *Research on Aging, 25,* 327–365.

Isaac, E. P., Rowland, M. L., & Blackwell, L. E. (2007). Fighting health disparities: The educational role of the African American church. *CrossCurrents, 57*(2), 261–265.

Jagers, R. J., & Smith, P. (1996). Further examination of the Spirituality Scale. *Journal of Black Psychology, 22,* 429–442.

Johnson, P., & Henderson, M. (Eds.). (2005). *Black Queer studies: A critical anthology.* Durham, NC: Duke University Press.

King, J. (2004). *On the down low: A journey into the lives of "straight" Black men who sleep with men.* New York: Broadway Books.

Leland, J., & Miller, M. (1998, August 17). Can gays "convert"? *Newsweek, 132*(7), 47–50. http://www.newsweek.com/id/122627/page/1

Mattis, J. S., Murray, Y. F., Hatcher, C. A., Hearn, K. D., Lawhon, G. D., Murphy, E. J., et al. (2001). Religiosity, spirituality, and the subjective quality of African American men's friendships: An exploratory study. *Journal of Adult Development, 8*(4), 221–230. doi:10.1023/A:1011338511989

Mezirow, J. (2000). *Learning as transformation: Critical perspectives on a theory in progress.* San Francisco, CA: Jossey-Bass.

Miller, A. S., & Stark, R. (2002). Gender and religiousness: Can socialization explanations be saved? *American Journal of Sociology, 197,* 1399–1423.

Pargament, K. I. (1999). The psychology of religion and spirituality? Yes and no. *International Journal for the Psychology of Religion, 9*(1), 3–16.

Patton, L. D., & McClure, M. L. (2009). Strength in the spirit: A qualitative examination of African American college women and the role of spirituality during college. *Journal of Negro Education, 78*(1), 42–54.

Riggins, R. K., McNeal, C., & Herndon, M. K. (2008). The role of spirituality among African-American college males attending a historically Black university. *College Student Journal, 42*(1), 70–81.

Shannon, D. K., Oakes, K. E., Scheers, N. J., Richardson, F. J., & Stills, A. B. (2012). Religious beliefs as moderator of exposure to violence in African American adolescents. *Psychology of Religion and Spirituality.* Advance online publication. doi:10.1037/a0030879

Sheared, V., & Sissel, P. A. (Eds.). (2001). *Making space: Merging theory and practice in adult education.* Westport, CT: Greenwood Publishing Group.

Taylor, E. (2008). Transformative learning theory. In S. B. Merriam (Ed.), *New Directions for Adult and Continuing Education: No. 119. Third update on adult learning* (pp. 5–15). San Francisco, CA: Jossey-Bass. doi:10.1002/ace.301

Taylor, R. J., Chatters, L. M., & Levin, J. S. (2004). *Religion in the lives of African Americans: Social, psychological, and health perspectives.* Thousand Oaks, CA: Sage.

Taylor, R. J., Chatters, L. M., & Joe, S. (2011). Non-organizational religious participation, subjective religiosity, and spirituality among older African Americans and Black Caribbeans. *Journal of Religion and Health, 50*(3), 623–645. doi:10.1007/s10943-009-9292-4.

Tisdell, E. J. (2000). Spirituality and emancipatory adult education in women adult educators for social change. *Adult Education Quarterly, 50*(4), 308–335.

Tisdell, E. J. (2001). *Spirituality in adult and higher education.* Columbus, OH: ERIC Clearinghouse on Adult, Career, and Vocational Education. (ERIC Document Reproduction Service No. ED459370). Retrieved from http://ericic.syr.edu/Eric/

West, C. (2001). Black sexuality: The taboo subject. In R. Byrd & B. Guy-Sheftall (Eds.), *Traps: African American men on gender and sexuality* (pp. 301–307). Bloomington, IN: Indiana University Press.

Whitehead, T. (1997). Urban low-income African American men, HIV/AIDS, and gender identity. *Medical Anthropology Quarterly, 11*(4), 411–447.

Wink, P., & Dillon, M. (2002). Spiritual development across the adult life course: Findings from longitudinal study. *Journal of Adult Development, 9,* 79–94.

Woodyard, J. L., Peterson, J. L., & Stokes, J. P. (2000). Let us go into the house of the Lord: Participation in African American churches among young African American men who have sex with men. *Journal of Pastoral Care, 54*(4), 451–460.

LAWRENCE BRYANT *is dissertation mentor and professor of health sciences at Capella University, Department of Nursing and Health Administration, Minneapolis, MN.*

LORENZO BOWMAN *is a lawyer and professor of business and management at DeVry University/Keller Graduate School of Management.*

E. PAULETTE ISAAC-SAVAGE *is associate provost for planning and assessment and a professor of adult education at the University of Missouri-St. Louis.*

New Directions for Adult and Continuing Education • DOI: 10.1002/ace

6

This chapter examines the structural arrangements and challenges many Black male athletes encounter as a result of their use of sport for upward social mobility. Recommendations to enhance their preparation and advancement are provided.

Academic and Career Advancement for Black Male Athletes at NCAA Division I Institutions

Ashley R. Baker, Billy J. Hawkins

There are more than 1,000 member institutions of the National Collegiate Athletic Association (NCAA), and each year at the Division I, II, and III levels over 480,000 student-athletes participate in championship sports on these campuses (NCAA, 2015a, 2015b). Although the NCAA and its member institutions tout the collective success and personal development of student-athletes, there is evidence that Black male student-athletes persistently face challenges, limiting their ability to achieve academic and personal success. Research has shown that student-athletes in high-profile sports, more specifically Black males who are significantly overrepresented on the football and men's basketball teams, do not perform as well academically as their counterparts in the general student body (Eitzen, 2009). They represent only 2.8% of the undergraduate population at these institutions, but 57.1% of the football teams and 64.3% of the basketball teams (Harper, Williams, & Blackman, 2013). Athletic exploitation, hostile campus communities, racial discrimination, inadequate personal guidance and academic support, and social isolation are a few of the key contributors to Black male student-athletes' academic underperformance (Beamon, 2008; Cooper, 2012; Donnor, 2005; Hawkins, 2010; Singer, 2005).

Higher education and sport have been a means of upward social mobility for Black males, and many Black people believe that athletic ability is more important to young men than academic accomplishment. However, a fair share of Black male athletes have not benefited from the investment of their time and talents in sport. They have met challenges either to making it to the professional sport level or to obtaining a degree and gaining meaningful

New Directions for Adult and Continuing Education, no. 150, Summer 2016 © 2016 Wiley Periodicals, Inc.
Published online in Wiley Online Library (wileyonlinelibrary.com) • DOI: 10.1002/ace.20187

employment. These challenges are the result of systematic inequalities that neglect the holistic development of Black male student-athletes. This chapter examines how mentoring and career development preparation can assist Black males in completing their degree and becoming employed. It will also address the structural arrangements and challenges too many Black male athletes are encountering as consequences because they use of sport for upward social mobility. We recommend changes and additions to collegiate athletic programs to minimize these challenges and to improve the career preparation and advancement of Black male athletes. This chapter also elicits the expertise of adult educators to work with existing models that seek to address the educational and transitional challenges of Black male athletes. More important, critical to the success of these adult learners is the assistance of adult educators in developing an educational model that caters to their unique experiences these athletes incur on university campuses when they are competing and following the expenditure of their eligibility.

Sport for Upward Mobility

Black males can experience direct upward social mobility upon signing a lucrative professional multiyear contract with a professional sport league. They can experience indirect upward mobility thanks to an athletic scholarship, which gives them a high-quality education and employment opportunities through a network of alumni and donors. For example, in 2014, National Basketball Association (NBA) star Lebron James earned $72.3 million. Thus, a sport like basketball is often viewed as a means for economic and social mobility (Ogden & Hilt, 2003).

Although many athletes like Lebron have seen much success at the professional level, hundreds of thousands of youth and high school athletes will not reach that height. Yet great odds against stardom have not deterred young Black males from the pursuit of a career in sports. Although sport has provided many gifted Black males with financial success, researchers believe that young men's overreliance on sports as a means for upward mobility is problematic (Beamon, 2008; Hodge, Harrison, Burden, & Dixson, 2008).

As a result, researchers have explored the socialization process among Black males in sport. The findings suggested that Black families and communities have placed more emphasis on the drive for high-paying professional sports contracts than on other areas such as academic achievement and career maturity (Beamon, 2008, 2010; Beamon & Bell, 2006; Edwards, 1984, 2000; Harris, 1994; Oliver, 1980). Parents of African American athletes were found to emphasize athletic accomplishments over academic ones during childhood socialization. As the emphasis on athletics increased, collegiate academic performance decreased and the athletes' expectations for a professional sports career increased (Beamon & Bell, 2006).

Beamon (2010) echoed the consequences of overemphasizing athletic participation by citing lower levels of academic achievement, higher

New Directions for Adult and Continuing Education • DOI: 10.1002/ace

expectations for professional sports careers as a means to upward mobility and economic viability, and highly noticeable athletic identities. Previous research findings that have suggested that Black basketball and football players are more likely to enter college underprepared and less likely to graduate have reinforced the intellectual inferiority stereotype that has historically plagued these young men (Gaston-Gayles, 2005; Sailes, 2010; Sellers, 2000).

Structural Challenges at Postsecondary Institutions

Research has found that both traditional and nontraditional precollege measures are important in predicting college academic achievement (Purdy, Eitzen, & Hufnagel, 1985; Sedlacek & Adams-Gaston, 1992; Sellers, 1992; Simons, Van Rheenen, & Covington, 1999; Tracey & Sedlacek, 1985; Young & Sowa, 1992). Examples of these measures include demographics, high school grade point average (GPA), standardized test scores, parental education, and noncognitive variables. A major problem facing Black male college athletes, particularly those participating in football and basketball, is the persistent gap between their academic performance and that of their athlete peers (NCAA, 2015c). Their underperformance in college has often been attributed to their lack of preparedness for the academic rigor of college and a lack of academic motivation (Gaston-Gayles, 2004), Scholars suggest that closer interaction with faculty may influence athletes' personal and academic development (Comeaux & Harrison, 2007).

In response to the poor academic outcomes of young Black males and their intense focus on sports, several scholars have examined factors related to Black male student-athletes' experiences once in college. Over the past 18 years, researchers have documented Black male student-athletes' overall college experiences (Beamon, 2008; Martin, Harrison, Stone, & Lawrence, 2010), their academic performance (Comeaux & Harrison, 2007; Harrison, Comeaux, and Plecha, 2006; Martin, Harrison, & Bukstein, 2010; Sellers, 1992), and their perceptions of academic and athletic opportunities (Beamon & Bell, 2006; Singer, 2005). Cooper's (2012) examination of the history of Black athletes' experiences at predominately White institutions identified four challenges these athletes faced on campus: (a) racial discrimination/social isolation (Adler & Adler, 1991; Benson, 2000; Hawkins 2010; Sailes, 1993); (b) academic neglect (Adler & Adler, 1991; Gaston-Gayles, 2005; Hawkins, 2010; Sailes, 2010; Sellers, 2000); (c) economic deprivation (Byers, 1995; Funk, 1991; Zimbalist, 2001); and (d) limited leadership opportunities (Harrison, 2004)

As a result, many Black male student-athletes experience negative educational outcomes, for example, lower writing skill, reading comprehension, critical thinking, etc. (Pascarella et al., 1999). These outcomes provide evidence that institutions are failing to fulfill their stated purpose of enhancing student-athletes' educational experiences through sport (Cooper & Hawkins, 2014). Cooper and Hawkins (2014) posit that this evidence compounded with the assertion that at many postsecondary institutions the social, cultural, and academic climates have been found to be unfit to meet the needs of Black male students; therefore, these young men find themselves encountering structural arrangements that are roadblocks for them but not for their counterparts. Examples of these structural arrangements include underrepresentation of Blacks in leadership positions on campuses—both within and beyond the athletic department (faculty, administrators, and staff), lack of culturally relevant artifacts and programming on campus, overrepresentation of Blacks on athletic teams and concurrent underrepresentation in the general student body, lack of culturally relevant curricula, lack of adequate academic support for achievement beyond the basic need to maintain eligibility and at times academic remediation and tutoring, and social isolation based on athletic team composition, living arrangements, and time commitments. Adult educators and other members of the campus community can help these young men overcome these challenges.

Student-Athlete Development Programs

Student-athletes need academic support that is sensitive to their athletic schedule; psychological support for their intense athletic commitments; and career development support. They have limited time for educational or social activities and are largely isolated from the general student body, particularly in season (Comeaux, 2015). Since the early 1900s, university officials and the NCAA have established policies and programs intended to improve the lives and experiences of student-athletes; however, athletic advising and counseling programs historically concentrated on academic eligibility and graduation success with less emphasis on personal development (Howard-Hamilton & Sina, 2001; Lottes, 1991; Watt & Moore, 2001).

In recognition of the student-athletes' unique needs, support services now extend beyond traditional academic advising, scheduling, and tutoring. At many NCAA member institutions, services have expanded to include developmental areas, such as career planning, fiscal management, nutrition, performance enhancement, and mental health. We discuss examples of programs next, including a newly developed program aimed at enhancing Black male student-athletes' experiences and outcomes within and beyond college.

CHAMPS/Life Skills Program. Challenging Athletes' Minds for Personal Success (CHAMPS)/Life Skills Program was a collaboration between the NCAA Foundation and the Division IA Athletic Directors' Association created in 1994 to support student-athlete development initiatives and to enhance the quality of the student-athlete experience. The program had multiple components: (a) the Academic Commitment; (b) the Career Development Commitment; (c) the Personal Development Commitment; (d) the Service Commitment; and (e) the Athletics Commitment. Participating institutions could access resources, such as program guides, books, DVDs, and promotional materials, to assist in the implementation of the program. In 2014, the

NCAA Life Skills initiative replaced the CHAMPS/Life Skills Program, and in 2016 the NCAA will partner with the National Association of Academic Advisors for Athletics (N4A) for oversight and operation of programming for student-athletes and life skills professionals at NCAA member institutions. The programming provided seeks to "fully prepare student-athletes for life, arming them with skills that are useful through college and after graduation. Customized education, tailored programming and engaging speakers address topics such as values identification, character building, financial literacy, mental health, community service, transitioning to life after college and differing leadership styles" (NCAA, 2015d, para. 8). This initiative provides Black male athletes with relevant programming that can help them navigate the academic and social cultures of the institution, therefore reducing the chance of alienation and better equipping them with the skills necessary to obtain a college degree and achieve gainful employment.

Scholar-Baller. Endorsed by the NCAA and established in 1995, Scholar-Baller is a nonprofit organization that has presented culturally relevant incentive-based educational programs for student-athletes to bridge the gap between education, sport, and popular culture (Harrison et al., 2010). Although Scholar-Baller is primarily focused on recognizing student-athletes' academic achievements, the program's commitment to altering student-athletes' perceptions about education, sport, and career aspirations has produced favorable outcomes in student retention and student-athlete self- and social identity (Comeaux, 2010b; Harrison et al., 2010).

Excellence Beyond Athletics. The Excellence Beyond Athletics (EBA) approach is a series of recommendations for enhancing both academic achievement and holistic development. Its purpose is to "empower, educate, and inspire students of color (athletes and nonathletes) to maximize their full potential as holistic individuals both within and beyond athletic contexts" (Cooper, 2015, p.11). The key components include six holistic development principles, two of which are relevant to this discussion: active mentorship and career aspirations.

Cooper (2015) suggested a formal faculty–student mentorship program as one approach to active mentorship. The program would include participant surveys to match mentor and mentee, mentoring training, and weekly mentor–student meetings. Kelly and Dixon (2014) recommended constellation mentoring, "a model that incorporates several mentors that meet different needs and in a sense make up a 'personal board of directors' for the student-athlete" (p. 509). Mentor pairings of family, peers, faculty, coaches, administrators, and community leaders would meet the needs of Black male student-athletes for psychosocial support, career development, nonathletic identity enhancement, spiritual guidance, etc. (Cooper, 2015).

The second holistic development principle, career aspirations, aims to expose Black male student-athletes to role models in careers other than sports. Career Aspirations attempts to counter the societal, often internalized, belief that professional sports is the best career path for Black males (Edwards, 2000;

Harrison, Harrison, & Moore, 2002). Exploring different occupations would expose Black male student-athletes to a range of career opportunities through collaboration between the athletics department, career services, academic advising staff, and other members of the campus community (Cooper, 2015).

The three programs described here are just a few examples of expanded support programs that address the needs of college student-athletes and minimize the challenges they face due to the demands of sports participation. Nonetheless, broad-based programs are limited because they do not exclusively focus on the challenges Black male student-athletes face. Black student athletes are more likely to be first-generation college students (Ortagus & Merson, 2015); to enroll in college with lower socioeconomic status (Hawkins, 2010); to have lower high school grade point averages; and to earn lower GPAs in college (Harrison, Comeaux, & Plecha, 2006). They experience academic clustering defined as the occurrence of 25% or more of a single athletic team enrolled into a major (Fountain & Finley, 2011); encounter the pervasive stereotype of Black intellectual inferiority and athletic superiority; (Comeaux, 2010b; Lawrence, Harrison, & Stone, 2009); and experience discrimination from faculty, coaches, and peers based on their race and athletic status compared to their non-Black peers (Brooks & Althouse, 2013; Cooper, 2012). These limitations require programming designed to empower Black male student-athletes and to develop them holistically. One area that shows promise, as Cooper (2015) has addressed, is active, culturally relevant, and meaningful mentorship.

Mentorship

Research studies on mentoring in the context of college athletics have found that mentoring relationships with faculty benefited academic outcomes and retention (Carter & Hart, 2010; Comeaux, 2010a, Comeaux & Harrison, 2006, 2007; Gayles & Hu, 2009; Martin, Harrison, Bukstein, 2010; Perna, Zaichikowsky, & Bockneck, 1996). A growing number of mentor programs give opportunities for educators, administrators, coaches, and practitioners to assist Black male youth in understanding the value and respect of accomplishments outside of sport (Martin et al., 2010). Taking into consideration the challenges Black male student-athletes face, Carter and Hart (2010) suggested that mentoring "could prove a worthy option for academic, social, and athletic achievement" (p. 383).

Martin, Harrison, and Bukstein (2010) defined mentoring as "the process of engagement in which an inexperienced person is guided by one of experience and expertise, and as a result a committed relationship forms that facilitates the achievement of specific goals" (p. 278). Using data from the Cooperative Institutional Research Program's (CIRP) 2000 freshman survey and 2004 follow-up survey, Harrison, Comeaux, and Plecha (2006) investigated the role of the "intellectual" as a mentor to male football and basketball players. Findings revealed that faculty–student interaction was positively correlated with academic, professional, and personal factors for achievement. In 2007, Comeaux and Harrison explored the relationship between male Black and White student-athletes and faculty. The findings suggested that precollege characteristics and the college environment affected White and Black student-athletes' academic outcomes differently and that the lower academic credentials of Black male student-athletes entering college supported the need for intervention. Although evidence suggested that faculty intervention affected academic success of the football and men's basketball players, the authors speculated that the limited interaction of Black athletes with faculty could be the result of the alienation Black students felt on college campuses (Comeaux & Harrison, 2007).

Comeaux's (2010a) study piloted a faculty-student mentor program at a large Division I university and explored how the self-rated academic and athletic identity of male student-athletes in the sport of football changed over the first year. As part of the program. the faculty mentor and student-athlete met at least weekly to discuss personal, academic, and professional issues. The purpose of the faculty–student mentor program was to (a) enhance student-athlete satisfaction with the college experience, (b) increase the likelihood of student-athlete persistence, (c) foster a better understanding of the roles of college student-athletes among faculty, (d) expose student-athletes to the larger college community, and (e) expose faculty to the athletic subculture (Comeaux, 2010b). As a result of their mentor sessions, some student-athletes who participated felt more academically focused, were more optimistic about their futures, and expressed a willingness to discuss their career aspirations. Thus, Comeaux concluded that mentoring as an intervention strategy had positively influenced the first-year student-athletes' academic and future goals and should continue to be explored.

Programs that establish mentoring relationships between faculty and student-athletes have proven to be beneficial. These relationships must continue to be cultivated on college campuses throughout the United States. Program directors should acknowledge the unique needs of Black male student-athletes and whose behaviors are highly regulated by NCAA and institutional actors. Athletic performance determines in varying degrees whether student-athletes continue at school. Black athletes do not have the advantages of their nonathlete Black peers who can both work and attend college, because their time is dedicated to athletics and performance is tied to their scholarships. Adult educators and practitioners who interact with Black male student-athletes in spaces that reach beyond athletics are encouraged to engage as mentors for these young men. Recommendations are discussed in the following section.

Implications for Practice for Adult Educators

According to the *2009–2010 NCAA Student-Athlete Race and Ethnicity Report*, Black males make up a significant percentage of the multibillion-dollar intercollegiate athletics industry, accounting for 60.9% of Division I basketball players and 45.8% of Division I football players (Zgonc, 2010). They comprise the majority of the athletic labor force at predominantly White NCAA Division I institutions (Hawkins, 2010). Many of these student-athletes are arriving at these universities less prepared than their counterparts for the academic rigor required by many degree programs. Once on campus, they face the challenges of being marginalized and stereotyped as "dumb jocks." Along the way, there are so many roadblocks to the development of their academic talent and identities outside of athletics. Despite the academic challenges they encounter, the outcomes of the positive connections they have with faculty mentors suggest a greater need for effective intervention. Making meaningful connections across campus increases the likelihood that these young men will complete their degrees and find rewarding careers. A wide range of faculty mentoring that attends to the needs of Black male student athletes is one way adult educators can create supportive environments for these young men. Mentoring is effective in helping them to transition into college and supports and assists students who have completed their eligibility but have not graduated with a degree. Even after completing their degree programs, many of these athletes become adult learners in need of additional mentoring and skills to adequately apply the content of their degree program to a career.

Structured mentorship programs created by the NCAA and implemented within the athletics department are beneficial; however, additional programs outside the athletics department can also address the unique needs of Black male student-athletes. Collaboration between administrators within the athletics department, adult educators, and other influential people on campus must be encouraged when creating programs to provide support for these developing young men.

Adult educators as mentors should expose Black male student-athletes to relevant and achievement-specific strategies to overcome the many challenges they will face as they navigate the roles of student and athlete. In order to do this, adult educators must acknowledge the role that athletics plays in the lives of these young men and be fully aware of the stereotypes they face as a result. Training workshops that provide a better understanding of the complexities of the Black male student-athletes' experiences with race and racism are imperative. For example, as Cooper (2015) suggested, written reflective activities for Black male student-athletes that encourage the identification of the racial microaggressions they face on campus is one way to better understand the racialized experiences these young men face. Mentoring programs should be designed to address the individual and collective needs of these student-athletes. It is also important to provide Black male student-athletes with an opportunity to be involved in the development of such mentor–mentee relationships.

Another contribution adult educators can contribute to this population is in working with the likes of the aforementioned programs, athletic departments, and the NCAA to strengthen the effectiveness of these programmatic

New Directions for Adult and Continuing Education • DOI: 10.1002/ace

efforts. Adult educators could also contribute in developing a model that is unique to the challenges this population of adult learners. Because a large majority of these athletes will transition into the workforce, acquiring appropriate skills to make this transition seamless is important. Because career preparation and development have been noted to be lacking among some collegiate athletes (see e.g., Stepp-McCormick, 2014), the expertise of adult educators can address this lack and fill this gap with assistance in addressing issues of literacy and the acquisition of job skills to enhance this population success in the workplace.

In conclusion, programs like Scholar-Baller and the NCAA's Life Skills Program, along with the Excellence Beyond Athletics approach, are currently creating more inclusive spaces for growth and development of student-athletes as a whole. However, it is imperative that adult educators and other leaders on campus answer the call for more positive mentorship of Black male student-athletes and program development to meet their educational needs and their transition into the workforce; mentorship and programs that develop them as scholars, athletes, and future professionals either within or outside of the sports realm. Theodore Roosevelt is noted for saying that "sport makes boys into men," and we can agree that physically this statement has some validity; however, in making holistic men it will take the assistance of practitioners beyond athletic departments. Adult educators can play a critically important role in enhancing the experience of Black male student-athletes while they are in college and well beyond.

References

Adler, P. A., & Adler, P. (1991). *Backboards and blackboards: College athletics and role engulfment.* New York: Columbia University Press.

Beamon, K. K. (2008). "Used goods:" Former African American college student-athletes' perception of exploitation by division I universities. *Journal of Negro Education*, 77(4), 352–364. Retrieved from http://www.jstor.org/stable/25608704

Beamon, K. K. (2010). Are sports overemphasized in the socialization process of African American males? A qualitative analysis of former collegiate athletes' perception of sport socialization. *Journal of Black Studies*, 41(2), 281–300. doi: 10.1177/0021934709340873

Beamon, K. K., & Bell, P.A. (2006). Academics versus athletics: An examination of the effects of background and socialization on African American male student-athletes. *Social Science Journal*, 43, 393–403. doi: 10.1016/j.soscij.2006.04.009

Benson, K. (2000). Constructing academic inadequacy: African American athletes' stories of schooling. *Journal of Higher Education*, 71(2), 223–246. doi: 10.2307/2649249

Brooks, D., & Althouse, R. (2013). *Racism in college athletics* (3rd ed.). Morgantown, WV: Fitness Information Technology.

Byers, W. (1995). *Unsportsmanlike conduct: Exploiting college athletes.* Ann Arbor, MI: University of Michigan Press.

Carter, A. R., & Hart, A. (2010). Perspectives of mentoring: The Black female student-athlete. *Sport Management Review*, 13(4), 382–394. doi: 10.1016/j.smr.2010.01.003

Comeaux, E. (2010a). Mentoring as an intervention strategy: Toward a (re)negotiation of first year student-athlete role identities. *Journal for the Study of Sports and Athletes in Education*, 4(3), 257–276.

Comeaux, E. (2010b). Racial differences in faculty perceptions of collegiate student-athletes' academic and post-undergraduate achievement. *Sociology of Sport Journal*, 27(4), 390–412.

Comeaux, E. (2015). *Making the connection: Data-informed practices in academic support centers for college athletes*. Charlotte, NC: Information Age.

Comeaux, E., & Harrison, C. K. (2006). Gender, sport, and higher education. *Academic Athletic Journal*, 19(1), 38–55.

Comeaux, E., & Harrison, C. K. (2007). Faculty and male student-athletes: Racial differences in the environmental predictors of academic achievement. *Race, Ethnicity, and Education*, 10(2), 199–214. doi: 10.1080/13613320701330726

Cooper, J. N. (2012). Personal troubles and public issues: A sociological imagination of Black athletes' experiences at predominantly White institutions in the United States. *Sociology Mind*, 2, 261–271. doi: 10.4236/sm.2012.23035

Cooper, J. N. (2015). *Excellence beyond athletics: Best practices for enhancing Black male student athletes' educational experiences and outcomes*. Paper presented at The Black Student Athlete Conference: Challenges and Opportunities at the University of Texas at Austin. Austin, TX.

Cooper, J. N., & Hawkins, B. (2014). The transfer effect: A critical race theory examination of Black male transfer student athletes' experiences. *Journal of Intercollegiate Sport*, 7(1), 80–104. doi: http://dx.doi.Org/10.1123/jis.2013-0033

Donnor, J. K. (2005). Towards an interest-convergence in the education of African-American football student-athletes in major college sports. *Race, Ethnicity, and Education*, 8(1), 45–67. doi: 10.1080/1361332052000340999

Edwards, H. (1984). The Black "dumb jock": An American sports tragedy. *College Board Review*, 131, 8–13.

Edwards, H. (2000). Crisis of Black athletes on the eve of the 21st century. *Society*, 37(3), 9–13. doi: 10.1007/BF02686167

Eitzen, D.S. (2006). *Fair and foul: Beyond the myths and paradoxes of sport* (3rd ed.). New York: Rowman & Littlefield.

Fountain, J. J., & Finley, P. S. (2011). Academic clustering: A longitudinal analysis of a Division I football program. *Journal of Issues in Intercollegiate Athletics*, 4, 24–41.

Funk, G. D. (1991). *Major violation: The unbalanced priorities in athletics and academics*. Champaign, IL: Leisure Press.

Gaston-Gayles, J. L. (2004). Examining academic and athletic motivation among student athletes at a division I university. *Journal of College Student Development*, 45(1), 75–83. doi: 10.1353/csd.2004.0005

Gaston-Gayles. J. L. (2005). The factor structure and reliability of the student athletes' motivation toward sports and academics questionnaire (SAMSAQ). *Journal of College Student Development*, 46(3), 317–327. doi: 10.1353/csd.2005.0025

Gayles, J. G., & Hu, S. (2009). The influence of student engagement and sport participation on college outcomes among Division I student athletes. *Journal of Higher Education*, 80(3), 315–333. doi: 10.1353/jhe.0.0051

Harper, S. R., Williams, C. D., & Blackman, H. W. (2013). *Black male student-athletes and racial inequities in NCAA Division I college sports*. Philadelphia: University of Pennsylvania, Center for the Study of Race and Equity in Education.

Harris, O. (1994). Race, sport, and social support. *Sociology of Sport Journal*, 11(1), 40–50.

Harrison, C.K. (2004). *"The Score": A hiring report card for NCAA Division IA and IAA football head coaching positions*. Orlando, FL: The Robeson Center and the Black Coaches Association.

Harrison, C. K., Bukstein, S., Mottley, J., Comeaux, E., Boyd, J., Parks, C., et al. (2010). Scholar-baller: Student athlete socialization, motivation, and academic performance in American society. *International Encyclopedia of Education* (Vol. 1, pp. 860–865). Oxford: Elsevier Ltd.

Harrison, C. K., Comeaux, E., & Plecha, M. (2006). Faculty and male football and basketball players on university campuses: An empirical investigation of the "intellectual" as mentor to the student-athlete. *Research Quarterly for Exercise and Sport, 77*(2), 277–284. doi: 10.1080/02701367.2006.10599361

Harrison, L., Jr., Harrison, C. K., & Moore, L. N. (2002). African American racial identity and sport. *Sport, Education & Society, 7*(2), 121–133.

Hawkins, B. (2010). *The new plantation: Black athletes, college sports, and predominantly White institutions.* New York: Palgrave-MacMillan.

Hodge, S. R., Harrison, L., Jr., Burden, J., Jr., & Dixson, A. D. (2008). Brown in black and white—Then and now: A question of educating or sporting African American males in America. *American Behavioral Scientists, 51*(7), 928–952. doi: 10.1177/0002764207311998

Howard-Hamilton, M. F., & Sina, J. A. (2001). How college affects student athletes. *New Directions for Student Services, 93,* 35–45.

Kelly, D. D., & Dixon, M. A. (2014). Successfully navigating life transitions among African American male student-athletes: A review and examination of constellation mentoring as a promising strategy. *Journal of Sport Management, 28*(5), 498–514. doi: http://dx.doi.Org/10.1123/jsm.2012-0320

Lawrence, S. M., Harrison, C. K., & Stone, J. (2009). A day in the life of a male college athlete: A public perception and qualitative campus investigation. *Journal of Sport Management, 23*(5), 591–614.

Lottes, C. (1991). A "whole-istic" model of counseling student-athletes on academic, athletic, and personal social issues. In E. F. Etzel, A. P. Ferrante, & J. W. Pinkney (Eds.), *Counseling college student-athletes: Issues and interventions* (pp. 31–49). Morgantown, WV: Fitness Information Technology.

Martin, B., Harrison, C. K., & Bukstein, S. (2010). "It takes a village" for African American male scholar-athletes. *Journal for the Study of Sports and Athletes in Education, 4*(3), 277–296. doi: http://dx.doi.org/10.1179/ssa.2010.4.3.277

Martin, B. E., Harrison, C. K., Stone, J., & Lawrence, S. M. (2010). Athletic voices and academic victories: African American male student-athlete experiences in the Pac-Ten. *Journal of Sport & Social Issues, 34*(2), 131–153. doi: 10.1177/0193723510366541

National Collegiate Athletic Association. (2015a). *Student-athletes.* Retrieved from http://www.ncaa.org/student-athletes

National Collegiate Athletic Association. (2015b). *Membership.* Retrieved from http://www.ncaa.org/about/who-we-are/membership/composition-and-sport-sponsorship-ncaa-membership

National Collegiate Athletic Association. (2015c). *Trends in graduation success rates and federal graduation rates at NCAA Division I institutions* [PowerPoint slides]. Retrieved from http://web1.ncaa.org/app_data/GSR/nablus15/GSR_Fed_Trends.pdf

National Collegiate Athletic Association. (2015d). *NCAA, N4A to partner on life skills professional development.* Retrieved from http://www.ncaa.org/about/resources/media-center/news/ncaa-n4a-partner-life-skills-professional-development

Ogden, D. C., & Hilt, M. L. (2003). Collective identity and basketball: an explanation for the decreasing number of African-Americans on America's baseball diamonds. *Journal of Leisure Research, 35*(2), 213–227. Retrieved from http://js.sagamorepub.com/jlr/article/view/606

Oliver, M. (1980). The transmission of sport mobility orientation in the family. *International Review of Sport Sociology, 15*(2), 51–75. doi: 10.1177/101269028001500204

Ortagus, J. C., & Merson, D. (2015). Leveling the playing field: Faculty influence on the academic success of low-income, first-generation student-athletes. *Journal for the Study of Sports and Athletes in Education, 9*(1), 29–49. doi: 10.1179/1935739715Z.00000000034

Pascarella, E. T., Truckenmiller, R., Nora, A., Terenzini, P.T., Edison, M., & Hagedorn, L.S. (1999). Cognitive impacts of intercollegiate athletic participation: Some further evidence. *Journal of Higher Education, 70*(1), 1–26. doi: 10.2307/2649116

Perna, F., Zaichikowsky, L., & Bockneck, G. (1996). The association of mentoring with psychosocial development among male athletes at the termination of college career. *Journal of Applied Sport Psychology, 8*(1), 76–88. doi: 10.1080/10413209608406309

Purdy, D., Eitzen, D. S., & Hufnagel, R. (1985). Are athletes also students? The educational attainment of college athletes. In D. Chu, J. O. Segrave & B. J. Becker (Eds.), *Sport and higher education* (pp. 221–234). Champaign, IL: Human Kinetics.

Sailes, G. (1993). An investigation of campus stereotypes: The myth of black athletic superiority and the dumb jock stereotype. *Sociology of Sport Journal, 10*(1), 88–97.

Sailes. G. (2010). The African American athlete: social myths and stereotypes. In G. Sailes (Ed.), *Modern sport and the African American athlete experience* (pp. 55–68). San Diego, CA: Cognella.

Sedlacek, W. E., & Adams-Gaston, J. (1992). Predicting the academic success of student-athletes using SAT and noncognitive variables. *Journal of Counseling & Development, 70*(6), 724–727. doi: 10.1002/j.1556-6676.1992.tb02155.x

Sellers, R. (1992). Racial differences in the predictors for academic achievement of student-athletes in division I revenue producing sports. *Sociology of Sport Journal, 9*(1), 48–59.

Sellers. R. (2000). African American student-athletes: Opportunity or exploitation? In D. A. Brooks, R. (Ed.), *Racism in college athletics: The African American athlete's experience* (2nd ed., pp. 133–154). Morgantown, WV: Fitness Information Technology, Inc.

Simons, H. D., Van Rheenen, D., & Covington, M. V. (1999). Academic motivation and the student athlete. *Journal of College Student Development, 40*(2), 151–162.

Singer, J. N. (2005). Understanding racism through the eyes of African-American male student-athletes. *Race, Ethnicity, and Education, 8*(4), 365–386. doi: 10.1080/13613320500323963

Stepp-McCormick, H. (2014). *An exploratory study of football student-athlete sport-to-profession transition: Searching for a comprehensive student-athlete career development program* (Doctoral dissertation). Retrieved from University of Georgia Catalog. (gua4273755)

Tracey, T. J., & Sedlacek, W. E. (1985). The relationship of noncognitive variables to academic success: A longitudinal comparison by race. *Journal of College Student Personnel, 26*(5), 405–410.

Watt, S. K., & Moore, J. L. (2001) Who are student athletes? *New Directions for Student Services: No. 93. Student services for athletes* (pp. 7–18). San Francisco, CA: Jossey-Bass. doi: 10.1002/ss.1

Young, B. D., & Sowa, C. J. (1992). Predictors of academic success for Black student athletes. *Journal of College Student Development, 33*(4), 318–324.

Zgonc, E. (2010). *2009–2010 NCAA student-athlete race/ethnicity report.* Indianapolis, IN: National Collegiate Athletic Association. Retrieved from http://www.ncaapublications.com/productdownloads/SAEREP11.pdf

Zimbalist, A. (2001). *Unpaid professionals.* Princeton, NJ: Princeton University Press.

ASHLEY R. BAKER *is a doctoral candidate in the Sport Management and Policy Program at the University of Georgia.*

DR. BILLY J. HAWKINS *is a professor in the Sport Management and Policy Program in the Department of Kinesiology at the University of Georgia.*

7

This chapter draws attention to the intersection of race and gender identities and their impact on the career development of Black men.

The Brotherhood in Corporate America

Tonya Harris Cornileus

I am a human resource developer with more than 20 years' experience working in corporate America. I am Black, female, and feminist. Over the years, as I ascended into higher levels of management, I became acutely aware of how the demographics changed with each rung in the corporate ladder. Corporate America is still largely dominated by White men, particularly in the senior ranks. What struck me was the steady diminishing of Black men from the leadership pipeline into successive executive management positions while Black women seemed to be increasing their presence in the senior ranks. The seesaw effect or what some may call the zero-sum game in corporate diversity efforts is what intrigued me (Stewart, 2007). I conferred with fellow human resources colleagues to find out anecdotally if what I was noticing from my personal experience was also taking place in their companies and across industries. Indeed, more often than not, their stories confirmed my experience. That discovery changed the focus of my study. Initially, I was fairly certain that I would inquire into the Black experience in corporate America and how race affects Black professionals' career development. I aimed to put the spotlight on how woefully inadequate career development theories still are in integrating race and the opportunities scholars and practitioners have to call for more culturally relevant career development. I was even more certain that I would lean on my feminist perspective to confirm what so many other feminist scholars have distilled, that corporate America is a patriarchal bastion where women, and particularly Black women, have greater difficulty achieving career growth and development. My own revelation prompted me to look more deeply into the impact of race and gender on the career development experiences of Black men in corporate America. Although I decided to center my research on their lived experiences, I did so with an eye toward how their career outcomes compared to those of their White male counterparts and to a certain extent their Black female counterparts as well.

Whites make up 79% of the U.S. labor force and Blacks comprise 12%. Of employed men, 35% of Whites work in management, professional, or

NEW DIRECTIONS FOR ADULT AND CONTINUING EDUCATION, no. 150, Summer 2016 © 2016 Wiley Periodicals, Inc.
Published online in Wiley Online Library (wileyonlinelibrary.com) • DOI: 10.1002/ace.20188

related occupations compared with only 23% of Black men, and of employed women, 34% of Black women work in that job category (U.S. Department of Labor, 2014). Black men are lagging behind White men and in many cases falling behind Black women too in the labor force. By 2050, Blacks are expected to make up 14% of the total U.S. workforce, but that growth is projected to be largely attributed to the increase in Black women's participation (Toossi, 2006). We have been inundated with reports of the high rates of Black male incarcerations, high school dropouts or lower college completion, and other systemic depressants that affect the vitality of Black men in America (Rosser-Mims, Palmer, & Harroff, 2014). I understand that some disparity in workforce participation is attributable to those realities. However, those explanations are not entirely applicable when you examine Black men in corporate America who currently occupy management positions and who have already demonstrated success in overcoming those societal impediments. Black professional men are twice as likely to be unemployed as their White counterparts. When employed, they have slower promotion rates than White men, are more likely to be guided away from general management roles having profit and loss accountability and they also earn 25% less, with the greatest disparity occurring at the higher echelons of corporate America (Grodsky & Pager, 2001; James, 2000; Parks-Yancy, 2002; Taylor, 2004; U.S. Department of Labor, 2014). I resolved there was clearly more to understand and that served as the motivation for this study. In this chapter, I provide an overview of the study and discuss the systemic structures Black men encounter in their career development. I delve deeper into those structures that repress their career development and the facilitative structures Black professional men employ to achieve positive career development. Readers will hear directly from the participants as they describe their career development experiences and outcomes.

Theoretical Framework

There is a lack of theoretical understanding of how the confluence of race and gender bears on the experiences of Black professional men in the workplace. The conceptualization of Black manhood, critical race theory, and career development theory provided the framework for the study. The conceptualization of Black manhood dates back to slavery. Black men were characterized as intellectually inferior and hypersexual, viewed with contempt, and thought to be incapable of being equal to White men because they were perceived to be racially inferior (Bederman, 1996; hooks, 2000; Hutchinson, 2002; Stewart, 2007). In this modern day, Black men are still subjects of negative stereotypes that have a lingering impact on the perceptions others hold of them and ramifications for their career development (Holzer & Offner, 2001; Moss & Tilly, 1996, 2001). The broad assumption that Black men are able to trade on their gender to gain privilege is misleading (Johnson-Bailey, Ray, & Lasker-Scott, 2014). In reality, the interlocking positional characteristics of race and gender have a cumulative effect of describing a man's hierarchical standing and

New Directions for Adult and Continuing Education • DOI: 10.1002/ace

experiences in America; and because of their social position as "Blackmen," being both Black and men, they more often encounter gendered racism (Mutua, 2006).

It is precisely the question of the impact of racism on the career development of Black professional men that led to the second theoretical underpinning of this study, critical race theory. The underlying assumption of critical race theory (CRT) is that racism is endemic to American society and serves to shape the realities of those advantaged and disadvantaged by race (Ladson-Billings & Tate, 2006). A core tenet of CRT is that those oppressed by race have a distinct voice or counternarrative based on their lived experiences. The findings in this study are given greater color by the examples emanating from the voices of the 14 Black professional men who participated.

The third lens of this study is through career development theories. Most major career development theories emphasize a person's capacity to make career choices. For example, one of the more influential theories is Super's life span life-space theory, which established the relationship of self-concept to career development (Herr & Cramer, 1996). The basic premise is that a person chooses careers that are consistent with his self-concept, and these choices are continuously made over the life span. Major theories have been routinely challenged for their applicability to people of color and women due to race and gender discrimination, socialization, and other cultural factors that affect self-concept and range of available choices.

There is a dearth of culturally relevant career development theories compared to the major theories, but they hold great promise in helping to shape career development practices for today's diverse workforce (Alfred, 2001; Hackett & Byars, 1996; Lent, Brown, & Hackett, 2002). Culturally relevant career development theories delve into issues of race, gender, culture, and context. A pioneer scholar in this area was Cheatham (1990), who through his heuristic career development model emphasized an Africentric framework to integrate the values germane to Blacks and inherent in African cultures. Cheatham believed that major theories could incorporate Africentric culture, thereby creating a holistic lens through which career development can be viewed for Blacks (Bingham & Ward, 2001). More research and theory development need to continue to establish comprehensive culturally relevant career development theories that support the career development of Blacks and other racially and ethnically diverse workers.

Research Design

My study involved 14 Black men, between the ages of 35 and 55, who had risen to midlevel or higher managerial positions in their respective companies. Through a series of individual and small group semistructured interviews, I sought to understand how they described their career development, the factors that influenced it, the impact of racism, and the strategies they employed to negotiate the impact of racism on their career development. I analyzed the data using the constant comparative method.

Findings

Participants encountered similar repressive structures and facilitative structures in their career development. A useful, albeit somewhat oversimplified, definition of the term "structures" refers to those social rules and practices that are properties of social systems created and recreated by members within the social systems (Giddens, 1984). Thus, repressive structures are those recursive social rules and practices that constrain the career development of Black professional men and facilitative structures are those that enable positive career development. Both repressive and facilitative structures include personal as well as contextual factors. The discussion of the findings includes participants' chosen aliases.

Repressive Structures. The four repressive structures found in the study included negative stereotypes attributed to Black men, subjective and disparate career development practices, differentiated acquisition of sociopolitical capital, and changing priorities in workplace diversity.

Stereotypes. One of the most prominent repressive structures cited among participants was the stereotypes attributed to Black men, which served as the basis for discrimination in their career development. Stereotypes are repressive because of their psychological and social component. It is how the generalizations, biases, and assumptions get acted out and form the basis of interactions, decisions, and outcomes that affect Black men's career development. Some participants spoke explicitly about the stereotypes whereas others only alluded to dealing with them. Each participant was consciously aware of the stereotypes and felt responsible for debunking those stereotypes for themselves and for other Black men. Henry Brown, a 50-year-old vice president with more than 28 years in sports production, described the presence of stereotypes in this way:

> I think the negative impact [of being Black and male in corporate America] has been constantly battling the myths, the stereotypes that exist for African American males...not smart enough to handle responsibility, not able to manage people well, not able to handle anger, just not qualified to be executive material. And so when you have to deal with that every step of the way and to combat those types of insinuations because nobody is going to ever come right out and tell you that. I think that could have a real negative impact on someone who is not mentally strong enough to process that and manage your reaction to some of those things.

Another participant, Bill Smith, a 49-year-old vice president with 27 years of professional experience, 20 of which has been in senior human resources roles, described some of the conversations he has been a part of when

New Directions for Adult and Continuing Education • DOI: 10.1002/ace

discussing career opportunities for professionals. He found himself regularly challenging others about their unconscious biases and attributions of certain stereotypes about Black men that were used to make decisions about Black men's career development. Bill stated:

> I think back to being in HR meetings or discussions where too often they were talking about African Americans and there would be these discussions of their style, and the reason we can't give them the next job is they are arrogant ... and it's the same thing the White males tend to get viewed as being confident about, so confidence becomes arrogance. And, I saw that very specifically in some of the discussions about Black males who had gotten to fairly senior jobs and the discussions about their next steps. They got viewed as having more flash than substance, and the interesting part is that I would always challenge them. Well, let's go to the record. What are the results in their business unit? Well, the results are good, but the person is so flamboyant. Well, let's not talk about how they got there and that's a different style they have, but the results are there. Let's talk about leadership. Let's talk about results. And, in many cases someone has to push that, but I'm thinking, okay, why does it always come up with us [Black men].

Gordon Sims, a director of diversity for a large utility and energy company, added that terms such as "arrogant," "flashy," and "flamboyant" are code words that serve to perpetuate negative stereotypes about Black men and discriminate against them. Participants shared that even positive characteristics have to be managed so they are not used against them. For example, being a go-getter or having certain degrees and credentials has also led to backlash or additional scrutiny. Steve Bell, a senior vice president in human resources at a media company, is highly educated. Having completed his undergraduate degree from West Point, he also holds an MBA and a doctorate. After a stellar career in the military, Steve has worked for several Fortune 100 companies. He shared how competence is still questioned for Black males:

> I think my color has also been viewed by some with skepticism. In other words, I've always felt like I'm going to get checked out a little bit more. It won't be assumed regardless of my credentials that I'm competent at my job. They are usually looking for some explanation as to why you are there [in the senior ranks]. I don't think an explanation is sought for others. I think as a Black male, clearly people are looking for an explanation in general for me as to why I'm at the level I'm at versus the White males that are similarly situated. I feel like my White male counterparts everywhere I've been have never had to deal with the same level of scrutiny.... So I think race in this case, this is how it's been played out. I feel challenged.

All participants were aware of the stereotypes and most believed their career development has been affected by them. The Black men were conflicted about their responsibility to represent other Black men, particularly when they are the only one in the room. Alfred, an organization development professional, sums up the conflict other participants also expressed. He asked, "I wonder how it feels to not have to carry the burden of my race?" He had vowed to release himself from the burden of always second thinking the stereotypes. He went on to say, "I think part of our dilemma is that we still carry that baggage. So sometimes we are able to move ahead, but we may hold ourselves back." His struggle was apparent because later in the interview, Alfred returned to this point, stating that fighting racism and stereotypes takes extra stress and energy to navigate in corporate America. It is something he said his White counterparts do not even understand, "It's out of their realm. It isn't even on their radar. They don't carry that burden. So every time I'm doing something, I'm not just doing it for Alfred. I have to represent my race."

Subjective and Disparate Career Development Practices. Career development practices include a company's policies or practices involving performance and succession management, hiring, promotion, termination, and selection to key job assignments and development experiences. From the participants' stories, I found the practices were rarely systemized and lacked objectivity, transparency, and accountability. White males were consistently top choices for strategic assignments, promotions, and leadership development programs. Only two of the participants thought that their career development experiences were comparable to or better than their White peers. One of the participants, Dallas Ward, a 38-year-old marketing professional and self-proclaimed high achiever, expressed that he had been able to achieve more than most of his White male counterparts up to a point. He found that once he reached senior director level, his career development stagnated while his counterparts kept advancing. He said:

> I see those people who have been on par with me, shoulder to shoulder, progressing ahead of the pack. We're both at the gates of the VP level, but I'm seeing more of them move to the VP level and I'm still trying to get there. I'm like, okay, what's that about?

David Minton, a vice president with a management consulting firm, concurred with Dallas. David stated that career development at his company is not based on performance, but on factors other than results. He said, "I'm getting better results than my counterparts, but I don't get the move. I don't get the promotions. I don't get the mentor." He added that once he achieved a certain level, he found he lost his sponsorship. He reflected that White male counterparts have sponsors at much higher levels in the organization and, as a result, they were able to gain more exposure to senior executives and their career development was able to extend beyond his development.

Bill, the human resources executive, stated that some of the biggest inhibitors to Black men's career development are weak succession plans, few assignments to strategic roles and profit and loss accountability, and not getting selected to attend leadership development programs. Without those types of career development experiences on their resume, Black men are excluded from consideration into executive ranks. The problem is that participants said they are disadvantaged because Black men are routinely left out of those experiences. Gordon, the director of diversity, who also spent time in the military, compared the career progression practices in the Army to those in corporate America. Gordon stated that in corporate America it is less clear about what it takes to get ahead, whereas in the military the promotion opportunities and requirements are documented and applicable to all and there is transparency. Conversely, in his company, managers were allowed to make decisions in silos and there was no open vetting by which managers were accountable for their decisions. Of the processes, Gordon admitted, "It does impact Whites as well as it impacts Blacks; it just impacts Black males more disproportionately."

Differentiated Acquisition of Sociopolitical Capital. Organizations are social and political sites. Social–political capital is gained when resources (information, influence, and opportunity) are exchanged among group members, and those groups are more likely to be racially homogeneous (Parks-Yancy, 2006). Parks-Yancy (2006) conducted a longitudinal study designed to look at the process of differential access to and career returns from social capital resources by gender and race. The results found that Whites have greater access to social capital resources than Blacks and were more likely to be promoted as a result of leveraging those social capital resources. Whites have an advantage because they have longer ties to corporate America than do Black professionals. The majority of the participants were first-generation corporate executives and they found they have a different access to sociopolitical capital. David, the vice president in management consulting, said he learned about corporate America through trial and error. He stated:

> They've [White males] been playing golf, they've been around the boardroom, the country club conversation, and I find that's a reality. They have been schooled in what they should say and what they shouldn't say and how to do the chit chat. They watched their fathers do it and the like. So, they have a tremendous advantage when it comes to that [politics].

Because Whites tend to have larger networks and longer ties to corporate America, Black men must gain access to White networks in order to develop sociopolitical capital that will lead to positive career development. Treadway, Hochwarter, Kacmar, & Ferris (2005) found that individuals likely to expend energy to engage in political behavior are those who see that engaging in the political behavior will yield organizational benefits (e.g., performance evaluation, pay, and promotion). To the extent that Black men are not likely to be in a position of power to grant the organizational benefits, they could find it difficult to gain access to capital held by their White counterparts for two reasons: their different racial group and having no sociopolitical capital to exchange. Thus, Black men can find themselves outside the in-group. Several of the participants mentioned feeling isolated and some provided clear examples when they did not have the same access to information as their White counterparts, had to meet a higher set of requirements to acquire a job or promotion, and were left off invitations to informal social gatherings. Jerome Felton is a 55-year-old division-level vice president in a financial services and data processing organization. He said his company still promotes people the "old-fashioned" way, which he described as accessing the network of relationships to exchange information. He said the process and outcomes for Black applicants are different:

> The problem with Black applicants is that nobody knows who they are so when they post for a position, because they are not recognized or acknowledged, they are not excluded because they are Black; they are excluded because they are not known. They don't have anyone pushing their resume.

The question then is why are they not known? Is it because they do not have the same opportunity to acquire the sociopolitical capital as their White counterparts? Bill's example is even more striking because it confirmed several of the participants' intuitions that their White male counterparts have access to information not afforded to them through social networks. Bill recalled being in a staff meeting with his manager and peers, all of whom were White males, and his manager asked him about a project that was past due. Initially Bill thought he had missed an e-mail because he was not familiar with the project. The manager became perturbed and mentioned that all Bill's peers had submitted their assignments. At first the peers remained quiet, but after the manager continued to reprimand Bill for not completing the assignment, one of the peers spoke up and reminded the manager that they received the assignment when they were at his house on Saturday watching the ballgame. Bill was the only one who had not received an invitation from his manager.

David said that earlier in his career he was not politically astute and it negatively affected his career development. Later, he learned to make conscious choices about when to engage in political behavior. He did not enjoy corporate politics because he felt his work should speak for itself without having to play those "games." He made a decision to leave one company because he refused to build social networks. Henry made a similar decision early in his career. These men later learned that leaving a company because of office politics is not a smart, long-term career strategy.

Changing Priorities in Workplace Diversity. Over the past 40 years, a major shift has occurred in workplace diversity efforts. The civil rights movement and ensuing affirmative action policies were catalysts that led to the diversification of corporate America. Amid social and political pressure, companies increased the ranks of African Americans in professional and managerial roles. Employed Black men, in particular, were in greater demand for prestigious occupations in the labor market. Between 1970 and 1980, the number

New Directions for Adult and Continuing Education • DOI: 10.1002/ace

of Black men holding executive, administrative, or managerial jobs increased each year at twice the rate of their White male counterparts (Collins, 1997). Today, Black men have gone from being courted and outpacing their White male counterparts to being the least likely to be hired or promoted (Parks-Yancy, 2006). The pattern follows that White men are most likely to be hired or promoted, followed by White women, and then by women of color. The changing priority is attributed to the erosion of affirmative action policies, a more diverse workforce, and flatter organizational structures. The result is a wider, more culturally diverse talent pool for a limited number of executive positions. Participants were disappointed in their companies' diversity efforts and how changing priorities have shifted the focus and the opportunities away from Black men. Dallas said he left a company because of their lack of commitment to diversity. Celica, a vice president with over 20 years in pharmaceutical sales, said the next time he looks for an employer, he will think about the culture of the company. Steve said, "I think nowadays for a company to not have Black executives in their ranks is an embarrassing fact." He, like so many of the other participants, talked about the changing priority and the impact of globalization on corporate diversity efforts. Steve said:

> The world has gone global over the past 20 years in particular and that trend is increasing. There are going to be so many diverse people in the workplace. If you don't have a Black male, so what? It will become less of an issue because you've got five Asians and three Indians. Nobody is going to get caught up in that … it's not the Black and White paradigm. I think that's going to be gone. I do believe the civil rights paradigm is going to be a dated paradigm.

The changing priorities in workplace diversity are repressive because systemically there appears to be more unchecked opportunity to exclude Black men in hiring and promotions considerations. The power brokers and organizational decision makers are mostly White males, and studies have shown that they have a discomfort with Black men and a preference for women when choosing between those demographics (Moss & Tilly, 2001). Black men have a tougher time making the argument of race discrimination if an employer has an otherwise racially diverse workforce. Historically, they have not been successful making the gender argument in a society where the male gender is thought to be privileged. The discrimination they face due to gendered racism is not widely recognized or accepted in law or practice (Mutua, 2006).

Facilitative Structures

In spite of the repressive structures the participants faced, they found strategies to successfully negotiate the impact of racism on their career development. Many participants enjoy a great deal of autonomy, are responsible for other employees and budgets, and are expected to develop and execute a strategy that has an impact on their companies' bottom lines. The participants stated that they have developed a set of tools and internal and external resources that help facilitate their career development. From their stories, five facilitative structures emerged: (a) the ability to build and leverage key relationships, (b) bicultural strategies, (c) self-efficacy and personal agency, (d) education and continuous learning, and (e) spirituality and purpose.

Build and Leverage Key Relationships. The ability to build and leverage key relationships was the most discussed facilitative structure. The relationships mentioned most often were family, mentors and sponsors, and other Black male role models. Through these relationships the men established their identities, developed their agency and work ethic, learned about corporate culture, defined their value systems, and garnered support and guidance in navigating their careers. When I asked participants what relationships stood out as being most helpful to their career development, they unanimously said mentoring. Studies have shown that mentoring relationships can have a significant impact on an individual's career development, including such advantages as faster promotion rates, greater compensation, and higher feelings of career satisfaction (Palmer, 2005; Palmer & Johnson-Bailey, 2008). Most of the participants' mentors were outside their companies, which limited the influence the mentor could have inside the company. Participants remarked how difficult it is finding a Black mentor at the senior levels but thought that relationship was highly beneficial. Palmer and Johnson-Bailey (2008) found "the relationship between a mentor and protégé works best when both share similar experiences and cultural background" (p. 46). Participants also thought that it was advantageous to have a White mentor. Alfred said if he had to construct a career development program for Black men, he would assign two mentors, one Black and the other White. Mentoring across racial lines is fraught with historical tensions. The reality is that Black men and White men have a history together that is a barrier to the development of a close, trusting mentor–protégé relationship.

Bicultural Strategies. Participants discussed their bicultural experiences of straddling between their Black culture and the corporate culture that is predominantly White. Inside corporate cultures, conformity is rewarded and that shows up in dress, language, and adherence to values, practices, and behaviors of White males (Ogbor, 2001). The bicultural strategies participants discussed most included internal and external resources. Internally, the participants established and leveraged an informal underground Black network and participated in company-sponsored affinity groups for Black employees. Externally, participants immersed themselves in Black culture through participation in church and professional and fraternal associations.

In principle, the underground Black network is not very different from the good-old-boy network associated with White males. The commodity of the underground Black network is information exchange. This type of informal social network is highly purposeful. It is designed to inform, warn, or help a fellow Black employee to be successful. Bill shared an example of an informal network where senior Black professional men gathered a group of junior Black professional men after work hours to share information about senior White executives, provide examples of experiences that happened at work, answer questions, and provide advice on how to approach certain leaders and warn against liaisons with others.

Participants identified corporate-sponsored affinity groups as one of the most helpful organizational structures that enable Black professional men to gain access to career development information and resources, increase morale, and build stronger social networks.

Self-Efficacy and Personal Agency. Self-efficacy, the belief in one's capabilities, is one of the building blocks of career development and the fuel that enables a person to exercise agency (Alfred, 2001; Lent et al., 2002). In turn, personal agency is the notion that people are active agents in shaping their career development. I found that the participants, above all, believe in themselves, shun the negative stereotypes, and have a deep sense of self-determinism. Steve's comment sums up their sentiments. He stated:

> I came from a culture of people who took action. In other words, they did not believe that ... you just stood around and you hoped things get better. You've got to take action. And so, if it's to be, it's up to me.

The qualities participants had that stood out to me were ambitious, competitive, strategic, and adaptable/resilient. Mike, a 35-year-old regional vice president of sales for a financial services company, and the youngest of all the participants, provided an example of the ambition resident within the participants. Mike said:

> Why am I going to get up in the morning and go to work if I don't think that one day I can be president of this sales department at my company? Why not? I guess I've always felt that it was possible. I think numero uno, that's just the way I'm hard-wired.

Dallas provided an example of the competitive nature of the participants. He said:

> I've always been one of these people that seize the day, takes charge of my career. So, I've always had this innate sense of I needed to be a go-getter and wanted to achieve. And I've had that ever since I can remember ... I'm going to be the best. I'm gonna beat you out. I'm going to be nice about it ... but I'm going to be the best. I've always remembered having that "thing."

Being strategic entails developing a plan for career development, such that participants made deliberate career choices about which jobs to pursue and which to avoid. Henry discussed building a 1-year exit strategy from his company when he believed he had reached a ceiling in his career development.

New Directions for Adult and Continuing Education • DOI: 10.1002/ace

Adaptability and resilience are qualities the participants demonstrated when they had to rebound from setbacks in their careers. Steve said:

> I can't emphasize enough the importance of adaptability. Things aren't going to happen as you planned them and so you have to be adaptable. So, the job may be different, the people may be different, the situation may be different A lot of times I've watched people and they get a map in their head and they cling to their map. I've always been willing to change the map and I think that's been very important and it has served me well.

Education and Continuous Learning. Participants stated that education has been their "ticket into the game." They engaged in formal and informal learning, and they believe that continuous learning has been a differentiator in their career development. Ten of the participants have advanced degrees and they learn continuously through professional development programs and key experiences. When I asked what advice they would give to other Black professional men, participants highly encouraged continuously learning through company programs, including taking advantage of tuition reimbursement, learning through professional associations and through selecting key experiences such as international assignments and job rotations.

Spirituality and Purpose. When I asked participants how satisfied they were with their careers, their answers focused on intrinsic values, which included such things as staying true to themselves and being authentic, being able to develop others, making a difference and leaving a legacy, and paving the way for the next generation of Black professionals.

David said he liked being in a position where he can support, motivate, and guide others. He said, "I like doing that where I no longer have to be in the limelight. I'm there automatically, but I can support other people. I'm not seeking the praise myself anymore." He also mentioned being at peace with his decisions on playing or not playing corporate politics. He said, "I stayed true to myself through all of that."

Implications for Practice

Through the counternarratives of the 14 Black professional men, we gain greater understanding of their experiences and structures that repress and facilitate their career development. I believe that this is a map for human resource developers interested in creating more culturally relevant career development. The men's stories should encourage HRD practitioners to engage in self-reflection to understand their performance in designing, managing, and supporting practices that lead to inequities in career development. Designing programs that are objective, transparent, and accountable should be a priority. Drake-Clark (2009) found that "because White privilege operates invisibly, human resources practitioners need to examine programs for evidence of hidden bias and to ensure that the programs are not operating in ways that maintain the status quo" (p. 135). This includes programs such as performance and succession management, eligibility criteria for high potential development and leadership development programs, job assignments, and hiring and promotion practices.

Mentoring relationships and strong networks have been shown to have positive effects on Black men's career development. Helping to facilitate formal and informal mentoring relationships and organizing same member affinity groups can create safe spaces where these men can express their racial and cultural identities freely and develop leadership skills. Training managers on unconscious bias and giving them the skills to create a more inclusive work environment are also important. The study is equally compelling for Black professional men, providing a guide by which to examine their own roles and biases and giving them strategies that enable their career development.

References

Alfred, M. V. (2001). Expanding theories of career development: Adding the voices of African American women in the White academy. *Adult Education Quarterly*, *51*(2), 108–127.

Bederman, G. (1996). *Manliness & civilization: A cultural history of gender and race in the United States, 1880–1917*. Chicago, IL: University of Chicago Press.

Bingham, R. P., & Ward, C. M. (2001). Career counseling with African American males and females. In W. B. Walsh, R. P. Bingham, M. T. Brown, & C. M. Ward (Eds.), *Career counseling for African Americans* (pp. 49–75). Mahwah, NJ: Lawrence Erlbaum Associates.

Cheatham, H. E. (1990). Africentricity and career development of African Americans. *Career Development Quarterly*, *38*(4), 334–347.

Collins, S. M. (1997). Black mobility in White corporations: Up the corporate ladder but out on a limb. *Social Problems*, *44*(1), 55–67.

Drake-Clark, D. (2009). *Discrimination happens without effort: How Black women human resources managers negotiate diversity in a corporation* (Unpublished doctoral dissertation). The University of Georgia, Athens, GA.

Giddens, A. (1984). *The constitution of society: Outline of the theory of structuration*. Berkeley, CA: University Press of California.

Grodsky, E., & Pager, D. (2001). The structure of disadvantage: Individual and occupational determinants of the Black–White wage gap. *American Sociological Review*, *66*(4), 542–567.

Hackett, G., & Byars, A. M. (1996). Social cognitive theory and the career development of African American women. *Career Development Quarterly*, *44*, 322–340.

Herr, E. L., & Cramer, S. H. (1996). *Career guidance and counseling through the lifespan: Systematic approaches* (5th ed.). New York: HarperCollins.

Holzer, H. J., & Offner, P. (2001). *Trends in employment outcomes of young Black men, 1979–2000* (Report No. JCPR-WP-245). Flint, MI: Joint Center for Policy Research. (ERIC Document Reproduction Service No. ED460180)

Hooks, B. (2000). *Feminist theory: From margin to center* (2nd ed.). Cambridge, MA: South End Press.

Hutchinson, E. O. (2002, February 5). Blacks still losing race to corporate top. *AlterNet*. Retrieved from http://www.alternet.org/story/12364/blacks_still_losing_race_to_corporate_top

James, E. H. (2000). Race-related differences in promotions and support: Underlying effects of human and social capital. *Organization Science*, *11*(5), 493–508.

New Directions for Adult and Continuing Education • DOI: 10.1002/ace

Johnson-Bailey, J., Ray, N., & Lasker-Scott, T. (2014). Race, the Black male, and hetero-geneous racisms in education. In D. Rosser-Mims, B. Drayton, & T.C. Guy (Eds.), *New Directions for Adult and Continuing Education: No. 144. Swimming upstream: Black males in adult education* (pp. 5–14). San Francisco, CA: Jossey-Bass.

Ladson-Billings, G., & Tate, W. F. (2006). Toward a critical race theory of education. In A. D. Dixson & C. K. Rousseau (Eds.), *Critical race theory in education: All God's children got a song* (pp. 11–30). New York: Taylor and Francis Group.

Lent, R. W., Brown, S. D., & Hackett, G. (2002). Social cognitive career theory. In D. Brown & Associates (Eds.), *Career choice and development* (4th ed., pp. 255–311). San Francisco, CA: Jossey-Bass.

Moss, P., & Tilly, C. (1996). Soft skills and race: An investigation of Black men's employment problems. *Work and Occupations, 23*, 252–276.

Moss, P., & Tilly, C. (2001). *Stories employers tell: Race, skill and hiring in America.* New York: Russell Sage Foundation.

Mutua, A. D. (Ed.). (2006). *Progressive Black masculinities.* New York: Taylor & Francis Group.

Ogbor, J. O. (2001). Critical theory and the hegemony of corporate culture. *Journal of Organizational Change Management, 14*(6), 590–608.doi: 10.1108/09534810110408015

Palmer, G. A. (2005). The career development of African Americans in training and organizational development. *Human Resource Planning, 28*(1), 11–12.

Palmer, G. A., & Johnson-Bailey, J. (2008). The impact of mentoring on the careers of African Americans. *Canadian Journal of Career Development, 7*(1), 45–51.

Parks-Yancy, R. (2002). Antecedents of managerial and professional career trajectories and their differential effects on Blacks and Whites: Gaining parity through human and social capital. *Academy of Management Proceedings,* 1–6.

Parks-Yancy, R. (2006). The effects of social group membership and social capital resources on careers. *Journal of Black Studies, 36*(4), 515–545.

Rosser-Mims, D., Palmer, G.A., & Harroff, P. (2014). The reentry of adult college student: An exploration of the Black male experience. In D. Rosser-Mims, B. Drayton, & T.C.Guy (Eds.), *New Directions for Adult and Continuing Education: No. 144. Swimming upstream: Black males in adult education* (pp. 59–68). San Francisco, CA: Jossey-Bass.

Stewart, R. (2007, August). The declining significance of Black male employment: Gendered racism of Black men in corporate America. Paper presented at the annual meeting of the American Sociological Association, New York.

Taylor, J. E. (2004). *The new frontier for Black men: A shifting view of senior leaders in organizations* (Unpublished doctoral dissertation). Alliant International University, San Francisco Bay, CA.

Toossi, M. (2006, November). A new look at long-term labor force projections to 2050. *Monthly Labor Review,* pp. 19–39. Washington, DC. U.S. Department of Labor.

Treadway, D. C., Hochwarter, W. A., Kacmar, C. J., & Ferris, G. R. (2005). Political will, political skill, and political behavior. *Journal of Organizational Behavior, 26*, 229–245.

U.S. Department of Labor. (2014). *Current Population Survey.* Retrieved from http://www.bls.gov/cps/

TONYA HARRIS CORNILEUS is the vice president, Learning & Organizational Development at ESPN, where she serves as an integral member of the senior human resources leadership team.

8

This concluding chapter discusses the important contribution Black men's voices have made and can make to adult education theory and practice. Particular emphasis is placed on troubling the various factors that contribute to the silencing of those voices.

Swimming into the Open

Brendaly Drayton, Dionne Rosser-Mims, Joni Schwartz, Talmadge C. Guy

In this current volume we've purposely used the title "Swimming into the Open" to signal that through the struggle there is hope and opportunity for adult Black males in America in which the field of adult education has, will, and must continue to play an important role.

Over the course of our writing experience for this second volume, we were met with reminders in the news media as to why we must remain vigilant in our efforts to expand the narrative around Black males in adult education and the professions. Therefore, the purpose of this final chapter is threefold. First, we aim to encourage continued dialogue and exploration around the important contribution Black men's voices have made and can make to adult education theory and practice. Second, we aim to challenge our colleagues to trouble the various factors that persist to silence Black men's voices in the practice of adult education. Third, we also challenge adult education educators, scholars, program planners, and policy makers to use the contributions in both volumes to inform their actions and interactions with Black males.

Yes—Black Men's "Voices" Matter

The unique positionality of Black men in the United States contributes to our understanding of the nuanced dimensions and interconnections of racism, gender, and citizenship. Three key themes in this volume are the persistence of racism, the role of positionality, and resiliency.

Persistent Systemic Nature of Racism. Publicized incidents of institutional oppression as well as covert practices and policies that exist in what might be considered arenas of success expose the pervasive ideology that Black men's lives are not of equal importance in a society that espouses equal access

New Directions for Adult and Continuing Education, no. 150, Summer 2016 © 2016 Wiley Periodicals, Inc.
Published online in Wiley Online Library (wileyonlinelibrary.com) • DOI: 10.1002/ace.20189

to life, liberty, and the pursuit of happiness. Although most chapters make reference to the historical and current ramifications of racism, Chapter 1 lays the groundwork for this volume through its discussion of race and racism and its persistent manifestation in institutional systems evidenced in policing and unequal access to education. The authors draw attention to the role adult education can and must play in addressing issues of social justice. The Black Lives Matter movement not only speaks to the actual valuing of physical life but is an umbrella term for the various dimensions of life that contribute to overall well-being as denoted in these areas—Black minds matter, health matters, and community matters. In drawing attention to the role adult educators can and must play, the authors note that the education of the individual, the community, and society at large is critical to advancing the well-being of Black lives.

Chapter 7 portrays the subtle ways in which racism and its legacy influence the career development of Black managers and executives. The narratives in this chapter convey that negative stereotyping and prejudicial practices not only constrain access to top leadership positions but create psychological stress and expended energy in fighting racism. The author draws attention to the legacy of racism in the limited access Black professionals have to sociopolitical capital resources, such as information, opportunity, and influence. In contrast, Whites have access to greater social networks through which they can leverage the sociopolitical resources that come from long-term ties to corporate America. The presence of successful Black men, including the president of the United States, Barack Obama, does not negate the reality and impact of racism.

Denial of the social, political, and economic ramifications of racism not only fosters an environment of silencing but curtails efforts to advance equal opportunity initiatives and thereby sustains systems of inequity and injustice. Garces and Coburn (2015) found that the affirmative action ban at the University of Michigan not only resulted in decreased diversity but "silenced the conversations around race and racism" (p. 843) and promoted a reduced sense of empowerment because the law no longer supported direct discussion of the issues. Stohr (2013) noted a 30% decline in African American students at the university. As one senior administrator noted, "a color-blind society is admirable, it is not a reality" (p. 843). Although race considerations are banned in postsecondary institutions in eight states across the country, the consequences of a race-conscious society continue to affect the lives of people of color—the lives of Black men.

The Role of Positionality. The social construction of particular identities can strengthen or minimize the value of other identities. Notably, the unique construction of "Blackmen" (Mutua, 2006) and its deleterious effects underscore the intersection of race and gender in the experiences of Black men. Chapter 1 explores the Black man as citizen and the relevance of DuBois' (1903) double consciousness where the perception and treatment of Black men conflicts with the privileges of citizenship in a democratic society. Similarly, Chapter 7 discusses the Black man as corporate executive and the significance of gendered racism (Wingfield, 2007) in challenging the assumption of male privilege. Chapters 3, 4, and 5 present the Black man as learner and the common challenge of overcoming substandard education, especially for those of low economic circumstances.

Chapter 5 also makes the connection between sports and academics—the Black man as the student-athlete seeking upward mobility through sports but must guard against the sacrifice of academic preparedness for team success and institutional public relations. The significance of this chapter was most recently displayed in the University of North Carolina's academic scandal in which athletes were given bogus passing grades so they could continue to play sports. And although we acknowledge individual culpability, we must take issue with the institutional mechanisms that would allowed this practice to continue for 18 years (Ganim & Sayers, 2014) and applaud the educator who exposed it. Chapter 6 offers a different perspective of positionality through a discussion of intragroup diversity. The Black man who is gay must address his spiritual identity in light of the theology of Black churches and community beliefs that are in opposition to his sexual orientation. In sum, Black men's experiences cannot be subsumed under general categorizations but requires consideration of their "polyrhythmic realities" (Sheared, 1999).

Resiliency. The experiences voiced in this volume illustrate that Black men created alternate pathways and employed facilitative strategies to accomplish perceived goals when the valorized or espoused pathway is littered with obstacles to success. Chapter 1 highlights a collaborative effort in responding to the Black Lives Matter movement through the creation of educational forums to address the issues underpinning the movement. Chapter 3 challenges incurring the high costs of a college education as the only path to success through the narrative of one young man who used the Internet as an educational resource to overcome a substandard education through self-directed learning and to become a successful entrepreneur. Chapter 4 offers an overview of how Black churches have historically and currently provided venues for meeting the educational, political, spiritual, and psychological needs of the Black community. In particular, they created an environment for training in church and community leadership. Chapter 5 discusses how alternate meaning-making strategies can address the conflict between grand narratives and individual experience. In response to sociopolitical barriers in the workplace, Chapter 7 explores the ways in which Black professional men enhance their career development opportunities through the establishment of social networks and mentorship.

These men are not simply consumers of knowledge but creators of it. They are not just simply path takers but path makers. This aspect of the Black men's experiences is often overlooked and overshadowed by persistent negative stereotyping. These chapters demonstrate the formal, informal, and nonformal ways in which adult education takes place and how they are employed by Black men to reach the goals they have envisioned for themselves.

When we began this project about 4 years ago, we had a collective understanding that the voices and unique experiences of Black men in the United States were missing from the canon of adult education literature but yet these men were present in our classrooms. We initially planned one volume (Rosser-Mims, Schwartz, Drayton, & Guy, 2014) but found it necessary to do a second volume because of the varied wealth of experiences and the void in the literature base. The struggles our authors experienced in finding resources for this topic speak to the need for continued research. As educators and practitioners, we are aware that the needs of Black men in education settings will be overlooked and misunderstood unless they are made evident. As we conclude this volume, we are even more resolute in our belief that for change to take place the lived experiences of Black men and their connection to engaged learning must be made visible. Unless we are knowledgeable of the students in our classrooms we are likely to overlook their needs. The varied experiences and the alternate paths taken produce different types of knowledge valuable in expanding our understanding of adult learning and education in general. We hope that the narratives in this volume have inspired you to take action through research agendas, the creation of venues for discussion, and the establishing and promoting of initiatives that foster the educational and social well-being of Black men and in essence demonstrates that Black Lives Matter.

References

DuBois, W. E. B. (1903). *The souls of Black folks*. New York: Bantam Classic.

Ganim, S., & Sayers, D. (2014, October 23). UNC report finds 18 years of academic fraud to keep athletes playing. CNN. Retrieved from http://www.cnn.com/2014/10/22/us/unc-report-academic-fraud/

Garces, L., & Cogburn, C. (2015). Beyond declines in student body diversity: How campus-level administrators understand a prohibition on race-conscious postsecondary admissions policies. *American Educational Research Journal, 52*(5), 828–860. doi: 10.3102/0002831215594878

Mutua, A. D. (Ed.) (2006). *Progressive Black masculinities*. New York: Taylor & Francis Group.

Rosser-Mims, D., Schwartz, J., Drayton, B., & Guy, T. (Eds.). (2014). *New Directions for Adult and Continuing Education: No. 144. Swimming upstream: Black males in adult education*. San Francisco, CA: Jossey-Bass.

Sheared, V. (1999), Giving voice: Inclusion of African American students' polyrhythmic realities in adult basic education. In T. Guy (Ed.), *New Directions for Adult and Continuing Education: No. 82. Culturally relevant adult education: Key themes and purposes* (pp. 33–48). San Francisco, CA: Jossey Bass.

Stohr, G. (2013, October 15). Affirmative action ban gets support at high court hearing. Bloomberg. Retrieved http://www.bloomberg.com/news/articles/2013-10-15/u-s-justices-show-support-for-michigan-affirmative-action-ban

Wingfield, A. H. (2007). The modern mammy and the angry Black man. African American professionals' experiences with gendered racism in the workplace. *Race, Gender, and Class, 14*(1–2), 196–212.

BRENDALY DRAYTON is the coordinator of the Guided Study Groups program and an adult education instructor at The Pennsylvania State University.

DIONNE ROSSER-MIMS is an associate professor and assistant department chair in the Department of Leadership Development and Professional Studies at Troy University.

JONI SCHWARTZ is associate professor in the Humanities Department at LaGuardia Community College, City University of New York.

TALMADGE C. GUY is an associate professor of adult education at the University of Georgia.

New Directions for Adult and Continuing Education • DOI: 10.1002/ace

INDEX

NEW DIRECTIONS FOR ADULT AND CONTINUING EDUCATION

ORDER FORM SUBSCRIPTION AND SINGLE ISSUES

DISCOUNTED BACK ISSUES:

Use this form to receive 20% off all back issues of *New Directions for Adult and Continuing Education*.
All single issues priced at **$23.20** (normally $29.00)

TITLE	ISSUE NO.	ISBN
_____	_____	_____
_____	_____	_____
_____	_____	_____

*Call 1-800-835-6770 or see mailing instructions below. When calling, mention the promotional code JBNND to receive
your discount. For a complete list of issues, please visit www.wiley.com/WileyCDA/WileyTitle/productCd-ACE.html*

SUBSCRIPTIONS: (1 YEAR, 4 ISSUES)

☐ New Order   ☐ Renewal

U.S.	☐ Individual: $89	☐ Institutional: $356
CANADA/MEXICO	☐ Individual: $89	☐ Institutional: $398
ALL OTHERS	☐ Individual: $113	☐ Institutional: $434

*Call 1-800-835-6770 or see mailing and pricing instructions below.
Online subscriptions are available at www.onlinelibrary.wiley.com*

ORDER TOTALS:

Issue / Subscription Amount: $ _____

Shipping Amount: $ _____
(for single issues only – subscription prices include shipping)

Total Amount: $ _____

SHIPPING CHARGES:	
First Item	$6.00
Each Add'l Item	$2.00

*(No sales tax for U.S. subscriptions. Canadian residents, add GST for subscription orders. Individual rate subscriptions must
be paid by personal check or credit card. Individual rate subscriptions may not be resold as library copies.)*

BILLING & SHIPPING INFORMATION:

☐ **PAYMENT ENCLOSED:** *(U.S. check or money order only. All payments must be in U.S. dollars.)*

☐ **CREDIT CARD:** ☐ VISA ☐ MC ☐ AMEX

Card number _____Exp. Date_____

Card Holder Name_____Card Issue # _____

Signature _____Day Phone_____

☐ **BILL ME:** *(U.S. institutional orders only. Purchase order required.)*

Purchase order # _____
Federal Tax ID 13559302 • GST 89102-8052

Name _____

Address_____

Phone_____ E-mail_____

Copy or detach page and send to: **John Wiley & Sons, Inc. / Jossey Bass
PO Box 55381
Boston, MA 02205-9850**

PROMO JBNND

Practical facilitation techniques tailored to the adult brain

Facilitating Learning with the Adult Brain in Mind explains how the brain works and how to help adults learn, develop, and perform more effectively in various settings. Recent neurobiological discoveries have challenged long-held assumptions that logical, rational thought is the preeminent approach to knowing. Rather, feelings and emotions are essential for meaningful learning to occur in the embodied brain. Using stories, metaphors, and engaging illustrations to illuminate technical ideas, Taylor and Marienau synthesize relevant trends in neuroscience, cognitive science, and philosophy of mind.

This book provides facilitators of adult learning and development a much-needed resource of tested approaches plus the science behind their effectiveness.

- Appreciate the fundamental role of experience in adult learning

- Understand how metaphor and analogy spark curiosity and creativity

- Alleviate adult anxieties that impede learning

- Acquire tools and approaches that foster adult learning and development

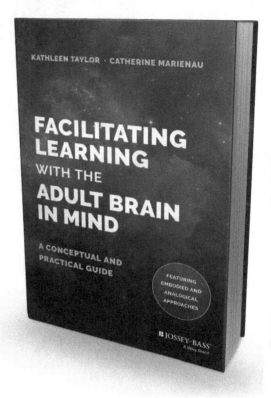

Also available as an e-book.

A Wiley Brand